Streak of Lean

Jimmy Reese

Illustrated by Ron Griggs

Cover photos provided by Jimmy Reese
(pictured) - An authentic country store with
hams and slabs of bacon hanging on the
walls.

Table of Contents

Dedication

My reason for writing a book, was to somehow leave a lasting memory of my family. I hope so deeply that this is what I truly do. I thought we were poor, looking back we were anything but poor. The thing I see as a common thread is that so many families and so many friends in my part of the world were living the same lives. I am as proud of my family as any person can be, and I stand behind them all. "Streak of Lean" will be a real time day to day accounting of what it was like to live as sharecroppers, growing up in the period around 1950 to 1970. I dedicate this book to the person who had the biggest positive impact in my life of anyone. My Grandmother, Sarah Ann Thompson Reese, 1898 – 1994 she was the glue that held our family together, if there was ever a finer person than she was, I never had the honor to know them.

Acknowledgements

Without the help of two people this book would have never happened. Pat Taylor Bullard and Ron L. Griggs. Pat and I knew each other in school but were never really close friends. We became acquainted again almost 40 years later on Facebook. As we were catching up on each other's lives over that long span of time we began to write emails which later became known as "Morning Coffee." In those emails Pat would ask me to make her "taste and smell the biscuits" "hear the sleet falling", describe the hurt so she could "feel" it. Eventually the idea for a book came to her, and she came up with the title "Streak of Lean" She tried to help me and get me to publish for years but I resisted. Ronnie Griggs, a childhood friend offered a couple of years ago to help me publish. He had just published his own book at the time. It only took me two more years to accept the invitation. Ronnie illustrated and formatted the book for Amazon and filed for the Copyright and ISBN number. Without these two friends, this would never have happened. Without my family and the life we were fortunate enough to live, there would have never been anything to write about. Without someone to make me realize that I was never poor, I was always rich, I doubt I would have ever realized it. I can't thank these two very special friends enough. A special word of thanks as well to Susan Bracey, who did the original copy edits and organized the structure of the book for me.

For You Alone

When all is said and done, and truth is finally
shown, and the soul that lives within, ascends into
unknown.
Thoughts and love and fears, we felt so many knew,
were shared by us alone, with just a precious few.
To touch another's life, and learn what lies within,
such trust is rarely gained by family, much less
friend.
When you can tell another, the secrets in your heart,
lay naked all emotion and fear not their response,
Then know that this is special, and revel in its glow,
for you have shared a pleasure, that few will ever
know.

Foreword

Dirt-poor is more than just a word when you live it day in and day out. It wears on your soul. Hard work is even harder without a dime in your pocket. You are never more aware of the haves and have-nots than when you "have not."

We were sharecroppers, farming tobacco, sometimes a little corn for animal feed and to grind into meal at the "Kenbridge Mill," ash potatoes, and a small family garden. The landowner, Mrs. Johnson, furnished us a house, outhouse, well, and a mule, the plows, and equipment that went with it. We furnished the labor and split the cost of all expenses of raising the tobacco: seed, fertilizer, herbicides, etc.

Luckily I had little time to ponder my lot in life. I had free range of the woods, branches, pond, and ditch banks that made up our section of the Plank Road, which appropriately was a red dirt road running between Highway 138, which we called the Union Mill Road, and U.S. Highway 1 down at Hines Store. The only rule I had to abide by was to be home on time for meals and the ever-present "you better come if I call you." I picked, ate, and sold to Mrs. Baisey, our neighbor across the road, blackberries and dewberries. Usually fifty cents for a quart. Good money for the times but it took days and sometimes weeks to get rid of the chiggers that always lived and thrived in blackberry patches. But I fished and frogged the branches and pond and dreamed of one day hunting the rabbits, squirrels, bobwhite, and occasional deer that I sometimes "jumped" while tromping the woods. I could mouth call a bobwhite and crow, and what a thrill it was when you brought them in "close" to you. Sometimes a fox would come when you called a bobwhite, which was rare but even more exciting.

I lived and ate most meals with my Grandaddy and Grandma. Went home next door to sleep at night but was up and back at their house by daybreak most times.

Grandma's meals, cooked on a woodstove, consisted mainly of fatback biscuits, butter biscuits, fried eggs, homemade jams and preserves (usually damson or pear made from fruit Mrs. Baisey gave us), and coffee for breakfast. Sometimes after a hog killing we had "middlin' meat" or what some folks call "streak of lean," a thick-sliced type bacon. Potato soup or navy beans for lunch and supper in the winter. And fresh vegetables every meal in the summer: sliced tomatoes (which my Grandma seasoned in a bowl with pepper, salt, sugar, and vinegar), fresh butterbeans, snaps, black-eyed peas, sugar Crowder peas.

Weekends always meant a special treat — homemade rice pudding, apple betty made from crab apples (again from Mrs. Baisey), coconut pie made from fresh coconuts, often a sweet potato pie, and sometimes a coconut cake.

Now and then we would get beef, which was a real treat; most of the time, beef stew, but sometimes cubed steak fried in a thick, rich onion brown gravy.

When we had fried chicken or chicken and dumplings, it had come from our yard. I never got used to the killing, and when I knew it was getting ready to happen I would usually find an excuse to go somewhere. My Uncle Page usually took care of the deed with a sharp ax on a big block of stove wood that had not yet been split.

And while seeing a chicken meet its fate was unpleasant, it paled in comparison to hog killing. Like most country folks, we kept a couple of pigs as meat for the winter. Trouble is you get used to them by the constant feeding of table scraps every day — "sloppin' the hogs" — and then acorns in the winter. Hogs love acorns and they will fatten them up fast.

My Grandaddy gave me a nickel for every load of acorns, a load being my red Flyer wagon full to the rim. A quart of hornworms in tobacco season also fetched a nickel. Hornworms ate large holes in the tobacco leaves and could do quite a bit of damage in a day.

As a farm kid, I usually missed most of the first two weeks of school, a blessing in some senses and a curse in others. I would not get to decide who my desk was beside and when the teacher "assigned" me a desk it would upset those who had already preordained their spots and cause underlying conflicts on occasion. Bus rides, lunch lines, the walk between classes, all those things had yet to work their way into my psyche. The sanctitude of summer, although drawing to a close, was still there. The farm had kept us poor, but it also had kept us together, and its peace and ease seemed   at   the   time   to   be   …   eternal

Reunion

It was the first week of September. Somehow it felt appropriate that our fortieth high school reunion was in the traditional week for the start of another school year. I had that thought on my mind as I made the drive from Raleigh, North Carolina, to South Hill, Virginia, my birthplace. In some ways it truly did feel like the changing of the guard. Like countless trips home before it, this one started at the same location. Color was just beginning to weave its way into the fabric of the early autumn leaves.

The place never seemed to change much: a huge oak tree in its center, with its myriad of limbs outstretched as if protecting those who lay beneath it. It was called "Crutchfield Acre," at least our section was. My Grandma's Grandaddy had donated this red clay ridgetop to the town of South Hill for a cemetery. It was here that I seemed to spend most of my time whenever I was in town, for it was here that most of my memories, most of my past, now resides. Plain field rocks, weathered granite markers, and rusted name stakes stand in mute testimony to the lives and hardships of those now below ground.

William Thaddeus Reese was more than just "1898–1962"; he was my Grandaddy, and he had meant more to me than anyone in my life during the scant eleven years we knew each other. The age difference had meant nothing; he was not only my Grandaddy, he was also my best friend.

"Sarah Ann Thompson, 1898–1994"; that doesn't do justice to the sweetest woman that I in my fifty-eight years on this planet have ever encountered.

Robert Chappell Hawthorne, Edward Jackson Reese, Allen Page Reese, Juanita Reese, Rachel Ann Hawthorne, Paul James Higdon, Mary Magdalene Reese, William Reese, Jr.

These are not the people history records, their deeds and sacrifices not deemed important by the powers that be. These are everyday people, the true fabric of society, and in all likelihood much like your family; my life much like yours. It had taken forty years but I had come to realize that we are not that unalike, any of us, rich or poor. The only difference in the races may be their skin color or the shape of their eyes, but not the content of their souls, not their wants and needs and dreams.

Like many of you, life for me has been more of a struggle than I could have ever imagined, and yet more of a blessing than I could have ever hoped for. This is a rambling, written timeline of one man's journey through life, chronicled both in verse and in text. An assembly of a life lived right; a life lived wrong; a twisted, tangled life that hard work and time somehow slowly organized.

Incredibly, it may be more similar to what we all endure on this planet than I realized ... or maybe it was just what happened in the six-inch space between my own two ears. After all, that is where our life is lived, is it not? What is real and what is imagined? What fears truly exist and what fears do we simply believe exist? Reality for every living being is somehow formed, lives, and dies in that small, often lonely, space between those ears. I am giving you the opportunity to enter and live in what was my world. Hopes, dreams, fears, happiness, sadness, confidence, dread, hopelessness, and euphoria. Come with me on the journey of a small-town poet. If you read this and are hurt, remember it differently, or feel slighted or demeaned in any way, please understand that it was nothing more than the weakness of the writer, the weakness of his memory.

I deeply loved my family; it took me a lifetime to acknowledge it, but no man has ever been prouder of his roots. This is just the way I saw it, the way my mind recorded it. Some of what I recount here was right, some wrong; the only importance, the only significance, is in knowing that we were a family, living in a microcosm of time, so fleeting and yet so significant. We were people, we had lives, we were a part of mankind, and we are almost gone ... and yet that in itself is the essence of life. As a man far wiser than I once said, "It's not what you take with you that counts, it's what you leave behind." This is what I want to leave behind: a written record of the brief period in time that the offspring of William Thaddeus Reese and Sarah Ann Thompson scratched a sharecropper's living out of the deep, red clay of Southside Virginia.

Through the Eyes of a Friend

I truly had nothing, it seemed,
Better days were no more than a dream.
Hand to mouth, one day at a time,
Hard times I thought, were all mine.
Money, gave everyone more,
No worries, no troubles, I was sure.
All changed by some words from a friend,
And once I looked back again,
Life's beauty, somehow concealed,
Sprung to life, like a mystery revealed.
A richness that I never knew had been,
Someone else had to see, looking in.

Jimmy Reese

Beginnings

I guess one of the blessings of our family is that we have always been very close knit.

My Daddy and Momma lived just a rock's throw away from the house Grandaddy, Grandma, Uncle Bo, and Uncle Lloyd lived in. Mrs. Marjorie Johnson, who owned the farm, owned both houses.

My Daddy and Momma's house was small, two-rooms. Clapboard, with no insulation, and sheetrock walls. The entrance was a small porch, and a tin roof covered both porch and house. The front room had a wood heater; big, round mirror with drawers on each side; a bed; and a small clothes cabinet. The second room contained a refrigerator, bed, table, four chairs, a woodstove, and a window fan. Two beautiful handmade wall cabinets that Mr. Peters, Uncle Bob's stepfather, had made us, looked oddly out of place among all the old furniture and appliances.

Aunt Sis and Uncle Paul lived about a half-mile away, in a modest four-room cinder block house with one bath and a big screened-in back porch. They rented from a man named Matt Wallace.

Uncle Page and Aunt Juanita, at that time, lived less than two miles away in a big two-story frame house with a large living room containing a wood heater, a couch, and several chairs. Next to it was a roomy kitchen, with a woodstove and walk-in pantry. Two unheated bedrooms lay at the top of a steep, narrow stairwell. Uncle Page was then sharecropping for a man named Frank Rogers.

Aunt Rachel and Uncle Bob lived in Kenbridge, in a small ranch-style brick house; three bedrooms, a bath, living room, and small washroom. Their house belonged to Mr. and Mrs. Peters, Uncle Bob's stepmother and stepfather, who lived next door in an almost identical house.

Mrs. Peters was a very refined lady, well educated, articulate, an immaculate dresser, and a stickler for proper manners. She oil painted, mainly wildflowers, and taught me to paint on old scrap pieces of canvas. She would make me take the time to clean up the palette and brushes, and always told me if I "showed talent" she would give me a real canvas to paint on. But that's another story!

Simpler Times

It was simpler times back then.

"What do you mean by that?" I've often had folks ask. Alabama in their ballad "Song of the South" summed it up wonderfully in four short lines:

"Well somebody told us Wall Street fell
But we were so poor that we couldn't tell.
Cotton was short and the weeds were tall,
But Mr. Roosevelt's gonna save us all."

Looking nostalgically back on it and living it are two different things. Living it was hard but looking back on it makes me long for those days again. I guess it's because now I know how it all ends. Back then it was just a day-to-day struggle. Thermos jugs were Mason jars filled with ice and water or on occasion Flavor Aid, an inexpensive version of Kool-Aid, and usually in grape or orange flavor. People made tomato wine or moonshine and sold both along with beef from freshly killed cows right out of the trunk of their car. Just drive up into the yard and negotiate a price or trade, sometimes a ham, eggs, streak of lean, cured sausage, or even a quilt.

Time was passed as a kid sometimes by simply turning an old car tire upright and rolling it along with your hand. I'm sure I logged thousands of miles at this alone. Wooden sewing thimbles were the closest thing to a real toy you had; stack them or roll them, the choice was yours.

You were more likely to get snake-bit or kicked by the mule than anything else bad; no cars to run you over, and no one to kidnap you. We cut what little grass we bothered to clip using an old reel mower, quite effective unless you let the grass get too high. Then you brought in the heavy equipment: the goats. Break-ins were unheard of, even in town. In summer, our doors and windows were wide open, day and night. Sure a screen door might be latched, but that was just to keep the kids from running in and out, and "letting in flies."

We ran a box window fan, but usually only at night so it wouldn't "run up the electric bill." I could spend half an hour just pressing my face against the safety grill, vocalizing songs, playing the old "fan harmonica," as I called it. It was one of the two musical instruments I could play: the radio and the window fan. The only reason we even used a fan at night was because with the daily labor in the sun that we did, sleep was a very important part of survival, and it's hard to sleep if you ain't cool.

That hard work afforded us another simple pleasure: food! We enjoyed huge meals, mainly of pork and wild game — squirrel, rabbit, bobwhite; fresh fish, fried in lard; pure butter on homemade biscuits filled with fatback; homemade jellies, jams, and preserves; cakes; pies; cornbread; beans; and garden greens and vegetables, heavily seasoned with large pieces of fresh pork, which were the most prized part of the meal. Flat, fried cornbread hoecakes — about the size of a Moon Pie — filled with sweet, crunchy, cracklings, again just slathered in butter.

And yet for the most part we were thin. We burnt it off in the fields. Sure there was the "Reese belly," but that was pretty much hereditary.

Sometimes at night if there was a breeze to keep the "skeeters off," we would lie on a mattress in the grass and sleep in the yard. Or at the barns in hammocks made from guano bags Grandma had sewn together. Sometimes we would burn a fire to keep the bugs at bay. It was pure joy to just lie on your back and gaze at the thousands of jewels flashing in the sky, reaching from horizon to horizon, with the nighttime orchestra of insects conducted in perfect harmony by an unseen maestro. Sometimes at night, outside on the mattress, Daddy would point out the constellations he knew — the Big Dipper, Little Dipper — and we would ponder the age-old question: "are we alone?"

Grandma made all her dresses from old patterns passed down and if a pattern didn't suit her, she could make her own pattern. All were hand sewn and finished off on the old pedal-operated Singer sewing machine that was her favorite possession.

Maybe Life is Simpler Than We Thought

if all the things I owned, were somehow bought and sold,
if I were just allowed, a few alone to hold,
only memories of family and friends, would remain forever
with me;
all else could just be scuttled, upon time's endless sea,
the things that truly mattered, the Lord gave those for free,
all else I chased and conquered, for me and only me.

but as I gaze forever back in time, the future never being
mine,
the present, in glorious halo glows, for it is truly all one
knows.
all else is rooted in might have been, or feared for, what
happens then.
the treasure never compromised, yet it was there before my
eyes,
all that I needed was set in place, boldly staring in my face.
but I was blinded by the need, to look for more than what
was seen,
to search in vain for the rest, the missing treasure from the
chest.
but in the end there comes a shock, the treasure lay in just
the box.
surrounded all our life with love, needing nothing more to
please us,
he gave us all just what we need, just simple love and
Jesus.

Land is Family Too

One of the hardest concepts for Native Americans to grasp, upon the arrival of white man, was the concept of ownership of land. Land and all the animals, waters, and plants upon it were a gift from the Great Spirit, meant to be shared by all people. Yet now a strange new man was claiming this land as his own, and the people who had enjoyed it, and nurtured it, for tens of thousands of years were suddenly no longer welcome. I felt the Native Americans were the greatest stewards of land we had ever known. They lived in a symbiotic relationship with all around them.

Land to my family was two pronged; it was joy and it was hardship. It belonged to someone else: the land, the house, the outbuildings, even in some cases the farm equipment and animals. Yet deep down, the land had always felt like it was ours. It was woven into the fabric of our very souls. We tended it, tilled it, fertilized it, planted and coaxed crops in it, and scratched a living from it.

Just off the right side of the house as you faced it from the dirt road was an amazingly level field of about one and a half acres packed with the most beautiful sandy, loamy soil you can imagine. The potatoes planted here overlapped the rows with their thick green foliage; harvest time brought bushel after heaving bushel of russet-colored behemoths, and months after digging, huge potatoes still surfaced. Any garden we planted here just exploded with growth. Tomatoes big as a man's hand, vines so packed with scarlet-red fruit the posts they were tied to leaned and sagged, like the masts of a sailing ship in rough seas. Fruit so full of flavor the juices would shoot from them when you pricked their skin with a paring knife to peel them. German Johnsons, Big Boys, Celebrity, Jubilee, and a luscious yellow tomato Grandma liked, that she called Lemon Boy. Its taste was on par with any red tomato but has less acid she said. She enjoyed it, and we left it for her. Butterbeans, fat and just about ready to burst from the pod when you shelled them. Snaps and sugar Crowder peas with oversized

14

shoots that dragged the ground.

One of my favorite vegetable dishes was one Grandma made from the snaps[1]. The pods would form so quickly beans would be bulging in them by the time you picked them, so she boiled them, beans and all, with tiny white potatoes the size of a fifty-cent piece. The end result was a coalescence of succulent, tender snaps surrounded by juicy speckled beans and mouth-watering, fork-tender new potatoes. I would drown them in vinegar and salt, and load me a big fluffy homemade biscuit with a thick slice of fresh tomato (just minutes off the vine), crisp crunchy fatback, and then pack it so full of butter you had to lick your fingers every time you picked it up. You can't buy that taste, you can't create it in a restaurant, and you can't forget it, you can't ever forget it!

Silver Queen corn would shoot forth ears so big you could barely reach around them, but still as tender as a goodnight kiss. Oh yes, we ate roasting ears dripping in butter and salt, but by far the best was fried corn. Grandma would shuck it, remove the silk, and cut the kernels from the cob. She put just enough bacon grease in the heavy cast-iron pan to keep the corn from sticking, then melted butter and poured it over the corn. Then, as it hit the hot grease she would gently sprinkle sugar and a little salt on it and cook it until it completely caramelized on the outside. It was then drained and served piping hot, bursting with fresh-picked flavor. There was never enough, you can't make enough. I was a fried cornaholic, and I didn't want treatment. Just more, always more!

Squash and green onions were just as bad. Correct that, just as good! Grandma picked crookneck squash barely out of its blossom, sliced it thick, fried it in bacon grease and with green onion bulbs, and then at the last minute added the chopped green shoots.

Uncle Bo liked fried okra, as did Grandma, but I liked it pickled: crisp, salty, packed with vinegar, and a cayenne pepper pod in the jar. If Grandma didn't watch me I could finish off a jar by myself.

Tobacco on this plot grew well over head-high to a six-foot man, leaves so big and thick they clogged the rows. The tobacco here, if anything, was almost too good. It was often hard to cure because of its very mass.

---

[1] Also called "Green Beans" in other parts of the country

15

Behind the house the land sloped downward toward a small spring and branch. It was still sandy and good land, but not as productive. Crop rotation was the reason; I had learned that in FFA, the Future Farmers of America. We had always just planted tobacco on the land and it would always have to be tobacco, because we had only about five acres so we couldn't change to wheat or soybeans in order to practice crop rotation; we would simply have starved.

Beyond the branch was "The Hill." The top section was hard-scrabble red dirt, which would sustain life but barely. Tobacco was lucky to grow knee-high to waist-high, with small leaves, and low yield. That land's only redeeming qualities were mushmelons, hornworms, and arrowheads. The mushmelons were fat, fun to hunt, and even more fun to pop — the muffled "thwoooop" as seed and spray shot from the end. Hornworms, hidden under the tobacco leaves, were thick as a grown man's finger; lime green, with rows of red, black, and white dots on each side; and the long black horn jutting out just over their eyes. They would latch on to your finger with the rows and rows of continually moving, viselike feet and hang on for their very life. A quart jar full fetched me a nickel and I never questioned their fate.

The Hill was also home to arrowheads; if you found an arrowhead it would usually be here. Arrowheads to me have always been special. They sent a shiver of excitement down my spine whenever I was lucky enough to find one, or even when Uncle Bo or Uncle Page found one and gave it to me. It was a genuine treasure. I would gaze at the workmanship and dream of what it had seen, what it had done, what its maker had looked like, what animal or man's life it had ended. Arrowheads were a time machine, a conduit and connection to the past.

The true jewels in life, though, are the simple memories we share with family and friends while we are still innocent. The day-to-day lives we live, when greed, hatred, anger, and lust are just words in a third-grade library book and have no meaning, no connotation. My memories of these fields and times still run deep. Grandaddy stretching to "top" a tobacco plant in the "garden patch" field, while I struggled to even see his knees, as I "suckered" the bottom leaves. Grandma in her faded headscarf and apron, basket in tow, brimming with butterbeans as she picked the

16

garden. Old Rattler, Grandaddy's dog, lying in the shade of the big oaks at the barn, lazily scratching the flea on his big brown ear. The sunlight glistening off the wet edges of a milky quartz arrowhead, its face barely peeking from the red clay dirt of The Hill.

Memories bought with love and tears, memories still recalled today ... with love and, yes, tears. Tears, the international currency of sadness, heartbreak, death, and yet new life and true joy. Tears are one and the same ... for man, woman, or child.

Memories

when my time draws to a close, and my sun is almost set,
what memories will I cherish, and which will I regret?

unlikely what I did, that garnered little gain, but what I failed to do, will cause the greatest pain.
people that I loved, yet somehow never told, waiting for the proper time, that never did unfold,
passed and never knew, true feelings held inside, untold truth is worse, than any mortal lies.

anger never fails to flare, yet love is sometimes hard to share, and often so is trust,
spend our lives together, and yet somehow we never, bother that true feelings are discussed,

and only when we're gone, are we truly known, too late to make a difference I suppose.
if we had only said, just what was in our head, what changes would it make, no one knows.

yet somehow it's a shame, when people hear my name, and don't know a single thing about my mind,
how I felt and thought, the battles that I fought, the love I held for those I left behind.

but it will never change, someone will feel the pain, the void of words yet somehow never said,
never knowing when they pray, that what they have to say, resembles nothing of the person dead.

our lives are so much deeper, than most can put in words, and even when we try, seldom are they heard.

there is no greater stranger, than the one plain in your sight, the one that lies beside you each and every night.

we all feel that we know them, and yet only when they're lost, are we truly made aware of what death really costs.

so lay your head upon your pillow, and do what you know is right, tell the one that lies beside you "I love you" tonight.

and if tomorrow you should awaken and they are no longer there, know that your love was taken, your feelings you did share.

your soul will be at ease, that's all that you can ask, till you will go to meet them, 'neath Heaven's golden stair.

Hard Lessons

I guess in certain aspects childhood determines the pathways of your whole life, what you are exposed to, how you see situations handled. It is then that the blueprints for life's lessons are molded in our brains.

Taunting in school was for me the most difficult repetitive aspect of life that I had faced. I understood and could deal with "poor." Sure, no problem. "Old clothes"? Acknowledged, got it. But taunting … I didn't know what you did with that. If you tried to rationally explain your situation, "cry baby" was the retort. If you tried to walk away, "yellow belly" was your response.

As a child I never really saw how confrontations were handled, and as a result my worst struggles in life have been in not knowing how to handle confrontation. I had been taught by Grandaddy and Grandma to just walk away. Maybe in the era when they went to school you could, maybe there was some modicum of respect in that gentle time, but not in mine and certainly not today.

We never really — thank you, God — had any real domestic situations. I don't remember any grown-up ever hitting another. I don't remember any arguments to speak of, maybe a few short words exchanged briefly but that was all. Sure there were the usual problems of any family. And alcohol may have been a root cause of some disagreement.

From my own perspective, what I had been exposed to was a progressive resolution for conflict. When simple verbal threats no longer worked, the next step was cursing. Cursing when done in an elevated depth and tone of speech, caused shock and, most of the time, results; the trouble is, cursing is rudimentary, Neanderthal. Whipping was the next step in the progression, but if the confrontation was not then resolved … then what? True violence, fists, feet, weapons?

I guess what stymied my maturity in handling confrontation more than anything else were whippings: the thick razor strap my Grandaddy used and the switches my Daddy made me pick. They were an absolute. Once you had reached the point of anger where a

19

whipping would occur, that was the finish, the absolute. Once you were told "no" and you sensed it was the final "no," there was no denying it; it was over. The situation then, regardless of what it was or however bad was, resolved through a whipping. Looking back, I think no worse lesson could ever be taught; violence in itself is not an end to confrontation in the rational world. It is, however, a delay mechanism, I suppose.

As early as elementary school I had noticed that kids grouped together by social status, although I didn't know that what was happening had a name. I just knew that poor kids played together, middle-class kids played together, and upper-class kids played together. As a rule, we were not mean to each other. Sure, there were isolated incidents, but mostly we just seldom mingled. I even realized it was because we could only identify with people of a similar lifestyle; we didn't share enough in common to form close bonds. It may simply have just been me, and an old thing called low self-esteem. But I was far too young to ponder thoughts so deep; it was simply one of those "it is what it is" scenarios.

All I ever wanted to do was make friends. These were people I had never been around, and we should be able to talk and play games and have fun, and we did not? I didn't understand that.

All childhood is cruel. It always will be, I guess. It is a learning curve for us all and it is for all intents and purposes still trial and error today, as it was then. All of us, rich and poor, were living in domestic situations that neither we nor any of our classmates could fathom or even had a basic working knowledge of. Ironically in a lot of situations, we all — poor, middle-class, and rich — were faced with the same situations at home. Had we been able to communicate outside of the cliques we formed, we would have found incredible friendship and lifelong bonds, but cliques constituted acceptance and safety. After fifty years to reflect on it, ruminate on it, autopsy it, I have unfortunately come to the conclusion that in many cases life all boils down to random chance, and in some cases confrontations are also resolved by random chance.

Dixie's Bridge

A Special Place

Reunions of all types, I mused, sure bring to the surface a lot of memory and emotion. High school reunions in particular, I guess. Looking at people I had not seen for forty years entering the building, wondering about their life's stories and the myriad of good and bad fortune that we had all endured in some form or another was draining.

I guess we all have a special place that to us carries a memory stronger than any other. For me that place is Dixie's Bridge. The bridge itself and the drive down to it are like going back in time in the literal sense and going back in time in terms of this life's memories, as well.

The Dixie's Bridge Road. A long, winding, narrow dirt road that strolls even now through thick woods broken only by small areas of open pasture. For some, I know it is not much shy of just plain ordinary, just a dirt road among a county full of dirt roads. Maybe that's why it's so special; maybe much like people, being ordinary has its charm, you just need to take the time to really look. As you gaze at rolling hills, you begin a slow curvy descent down to Dixie's Bridge.

Dixie's Bridge spans the Meherrin River. I don't know which was named first, the river or the Indians who long ago lived along its banks. But the name "Meherrin" means "people of the muddy water" and the river is usually muddy.

Dixie's Bridge is narrow. It allows only one car to cross at a time. Repaired many times over the years by Old Man Conner and his bridge gang, the bridge has a wooden floor with wide gaps between the planks, showing the river below and wooden bridge supports. A thin, waist-high iron pipe railing, about two inches thick, serves as the only barrier between you and the river below. It creaks and groans, and its rattling movement makes it seem alive as you slowly cross over. Every few feet is a big, bent piece of the rail, where someone got too close.

I would hear stories of how Grandaddy's daddy had pulled

cars across the bridge with his mule when the water got too high to drive across, of how the river would get so high you couldn't even see the bridge for days at a time, and yet when the waters went away the bridge would always be there. Mr. Connell had told me many times that Dixie's Bridge was "built right."

A ride on the Dixie's Bridge Road was the perfect therapy for a kid who had never been anywhere, or an adult who needed to get away from hard times and the stress of being without. When I was a small child, it conjured up images of what the mountains must look like. The cows grazing on the steeply sloped hillsides were part of a large cattle drive like the one we watched on Rawhide every week. Just beyond the herd, some lying chewing their cud, some meandering and slowly gleaning the tender green shoots of early spring grass, I could see in my mind's eye the smoke from the cook's campfire, wafting skyward just over the edge of the hilltop. Cowhands sitting around the big fire, noisily scraping kidney beans with fatback from tin plates with big pewter forks. Dirty, calloused hands wrapped around fat sourdough biscuits, being washed down with scalding-hot black coffee held in dented, scratched metal cups. Laughter filled the air as the stress from the hard day's work found release. The cook would be cutting hair, pulling teeth, and mending torn clothes as he waited for the meal to end.

From early on we had adopted each other, Dixie's Bridge and I. For me it had been a lifelong love affair. I have always viewed the Meherrin River and Dixie's Bridge as a land that time forgot, for it is today as it had been for my whole existence and, at least in my imagination, for thousands of years before that as well. Dixie's Bridge to me was so cherished, I would fight the Devil for it. If I could choose where I would die, it would be here on this bridge, with my family and friends around me, blending into and evaporating with the scarlet sunset of a cool fall afternoon.

Dixie's Bridge. It had helped me over and through the worst times of my life. And it had been there through countless celebrations and happy times as well. I had fished its banks and creek channels, eaten its bounty. I remembered a time when a young child ended the grief of a loved one here. I remembered an early time during the army, when in basic training I had put up with about all I could handle, and the thing that pushed me through to the end was the dream of one day again standing on Dixie's Bridge; of again being a free man with free will and able to make my own decisions and not be a GI, "Government Issue." Government Property.

In the army, things are one of two conditions: dispensable and indispensable. Toilet paper was indispensable; soldiers, people, were dispensable. They did not matter, they held no value. I had been threatened with an Article 15 military punishment for getting a sunburn while on a weekend pass. The charge, "defacing government property"; my body was government property, a lesson that remains to this day.

I struggle to find a way to explain the pull of Dixie's Bridge. To understand its magnetism, you need to experience it both by day and by night.

By day take a slow, enveloping look in both directions, then close your eyes, relax, and let the weight of the world drop from your shoulders. Take in a lingering deep breath; smell the damp river-bottom air, the tea-colored water, the thick jade-colored vegetation of the high sandy banks, the heady heart pine of the age-old bridge timbers. Feel deep in your soul the solitude, the quietness. Let the need to do nothing, to go nowhere sink into your heart. Enjoy the rustle of the overhead leaves as the breeze soothes and cools. Mingle with the spirits of the myriad of people who have gazed upon this very sight, lived hand-to-mouth from this very water, relaxed on these shady banks; let them reunite as a shared spirit.

By night the darkness surrounds you like a warm blanket. Screech owls and loons call out in songs so wild the hair on your neck raises its shackles. The high mysterious banks snap and crackle from falling limbs, the footsteps of the wildlife of the night as they start their journey. Pinpoints of starlight sparkle as they find their way through limb and leaf. Set free your imagination, leave it no boundaries, anything is possible here, it seems. Wolves, bear. I haven't heard one yet but a friend told me he has heard and seen coyote here; they are now migrating ever-eastward into the area.

In the final analysis, I guess what we hold special, what gives our life direction and meaning, what anchors us to our roots and our past is an intensely personal thing. Maybe the true beauty is not in the ride, not even in the final destination, but in the mere fact that someone else means enough to you that you want to at least attempt to share with them what has been so special to you.

Counter Factual Thinking

Scientists call it counter factual thinking; motivational speakers call it visualization. It is no more than the ability to imagine what might have happened instead of what just happened. Whatever you may wish to call it, I knew I was guilty of it, and it did not sit very well. I was not very proud of myself at the moment.

I had promised a special friend I would take her and her husband to this place, which for me held untold beauty and deep meaning, but as we went I worried if it would indeed be special to them.

In reality, the day itself could have been no more beautiful, and circumstances certainly could have made it no more pleasurable. Yet as I sat with my newest friends, staring at the smoothly worn head bolts of the rutted wood planking and rubbing the rusted steel beams of the old bridge, I somehow felt the need to apologize.

It seemed that the sight I had so long wanted to share with them was no longer there for me to share. What I had brought them to see now lived only in my own mind, I thought. Sure I could describe it, and I can without doubt still feel, see, taste, smell, and hear it, but it was no longer real, no longer tangible. The hearty gurgle of the clear, flowing creek, rushing headlong into the mighty current of the white-flecked, muddy Meherrin River was gone, nothing left but desiccated logs and limbs, now littering the steep sides of a bone-dry stream bed. The Meherrin River itself was no more than just a fast-flowing trickle on either bank, its center reduced to a wide sand bar and mud flat, with just mere inches of water flowing over them in the lower, luckier areas.

I had wanted for so long to bring Pat and George here to show them something that was special to me. I had envisioned us sitting in the cool shade, basking in the beauty of what in my mind's eye, was the Dixie's Bridge of my childhood. I would mouth call a bobwhite, or maybe a flock of crows I had thought; that would be a fun thing to do.

In the selfishness of my quest, however, as I often do, I had neglected to recognize that, really, all I had brought them to see was still there. Tucked among the mountain daisies and pawpaws lining the bank was the peace and quiet, the solitude and solace, the opportunity for uninterrupted conversation inside nature's cathedral. It was all still there, its magic no less diminished by the low water table.

Somehow mingled in with my emotions I felt maybe it was more appropriate that I apologize *to* the river, rather than *for* it. I humbly realized as well that we have grown old together, Dixie's Bridge and me.

Its once-strong current and depth were now reduced to just this trickle of water, its flow choked by the greed of man and the forces of nature. Drought today, as I'm sure it has for millennia, still ravages all areas at times, unchecked, in life's never-ending cycle. The hardest lessons to absorb sometimes are the simplest ones. I guess it really is true: "the only thing permanent in life is change."

Much like this river also am I, once filled with boundless energy and wonder, intrigue and excitement, unbridled hope and dreams, all now reduced to just a trickle of their own.

But life still clings tenaciously in both of us. In its ever-dwindling shallows, seemingly now threatening any day to depart, taking with it all life, fish of all sizes nurse a small bounty and struggle onward, waiting for the water to return. Catfish and redhorse work what is left of the rocky bottoms and the bank current formed by the river's edges, fighting it upstream and then drifting back with it, again and yet again, searching for insects knocked by wind into water. Small river chub minnows endlessly flit and flicker to filter the inches-deep water of the mud flats, seeking out the algae needed for survival. Am I any different? I don't think so. The spark is still there to achieve, to aspire, to fight to see the dawn of another day, to give it all one more chance.

I, much like the river, wait patiently for the water to return, but with the doubt gnawing at the depths of my soul, I, like the river, know it is quite possible that it never will. But maybe that is what draws me back, forever back to this spot that I have claimed as my own, for we have unfinished business, Dixie's Bridge and me. I'm not sure either of us understands what it is, but on this day my doubt in the old bridge and the river was unfounded. Maybe Dixie's Bridge in its own inimitable way had told me to cast my doubt aside as well.

On this day I will only cherish the warm memories made with new friends. I will let the river and the bridge mend its own soul, for its wisdom, its forgiveness, its healing, is far greater than that of man.

Grandma

My grandma, Sarah, was only about five feet two inches on her tallest day. Waist-length hair that she kept rolled and pinned into a "cinnamon bun" in the back, blue eyes, the sweetest smile, and the most easy-going disposition of anyone I have ever known. She had a fourth-grade education and yet, when I look back, I realize that she was far more intelligent than the majority of the most educated people I have ever known. She could handle the  most stressful situations with grace and dignity. She could not be panicked, and she could not be angered, no matter the situation. In what was an unusual trait, especially in a small town, she would not gossip and she would not allow it in her presence. Period. End of story.

"If you can't say something good, don't say any more." I have heard her say that in front of twenty or more people without raising her voice and it stopped. Right then. Bam. Over.

She would speak once to a child and whether they were two or fifteen or thirty-five, they would comply, no questions asked. I never understood her power. She had never whipped or even threatened to whip anyone. Her tone was always even, always low, and she always accomplished what she wanted without the whipping. Looking back, maybe that was her power, maybe knowing she would not whip you if you behaved?

She could feed a meal to whoever showed up, and it was always enough for everyone, and always great. Even though we were likely the poorest of the family, everyone would eat with Grandma on the holidays and she would not allow you to bring anything. That was her treat, her time, her enjoyment.

She had a woodstove, wood heater, cast-iron pots and pans, and no running water. She used a flat iron heated on the stove to iron clothes. She kept house, cooked all meals, cleaned all dishes, washed and ironed all clothes, and yet still worked in the field as much as any man, and she was still doing it at eighty-two years old. Never with any help. Even when we filled barns and her daughters and daughter-in-law offered her help, she declined. I asked her once how she did all that and her answer was "vitims"; she always bought a bottle of vitamins from the Watkins salesman, who in those days sold from the trunk of his car. I remember vanilla flavoring and "vitims" was all she ever bought.

She never drank, dipped snuff, or smoked but she did not look down on those that did. "Live and let live." I can hear her now.

She was deeply religious, but she lived it as her personal life and kept her beliefs to herself. She would answer any questions she could about church and the Bible but outside of a gentle nudge to "come on and go to church with me Sunday," she did not try to force religion on you. She addressed it as being a decision that you personally had to make with the Lord; it was not something you could be made to do or coerced into. When the time was right you would know it, and if it wasn't your own personal, conscious decision, then it just wasn't a done deal. I always had greatly respected her for the way she treated that aspect of her life.

Grandma did not miss church. Mr. and Mrs. Robert Morris took her to church, and brought her home every Sunday. She went to Sunday School and the morning worship service every Sunday morning, and if they were going Wednesday night, she again rode with them; they never failed to give her a ride. She was proud to be recognized as the oldest member of La Crosse Baptist Church and also proud of the fact that she gave a tithe.

She dearly loved Whitman's chocolate, and her children pitched in and got her a box every year at Christmas. She would always share it with me, but we could have "one piece each" every three days and never more, until it was gone. She would sit in her rocking chair sewing scrap cloth into "quilt patches" and we would just talk and eat candy, slowly. Some of the best memories and advice I was given in life to this day came during candy time.

Grandma loved to quilt and would work until her fingers bled hand-stitching some of the most beautiful homemade quilts I have ever seen. I still have one, and I love it so much I wish it could be buried with me, but then I would deprive my sons of a cherished heirloom.

And checkers. My goodness she was a weapon of mass destruction when it came to checkers; she could not be beaten. She would never taunt or tease, but she was merciless, and she would win. I honestly don't think I ever beat her and I'm not sure if anyone did. I never knew why she was so intense at checkers. But then she was intense … at all phases of life.

We suffered through so many struggles with money over the years, but when she died we learned she had saved more than $10,000 in her lifetime and she had, literally, done that with pennies, nickels, and dimes at a time. Selling a few eggs, homemade butter patties, an occasional quilt. She had told my Aunt Sis at some point that the money had been saved so "no one would have to pay for her burial." She had avoided insurance because she could not depend on having the money to pay every month, and the money she put in the bank, stayed in the bank. What a constitution! She could have made her life easier many times by just taking out a little and yet she never did.

We're Just Po Folks

Grandaddy was a big man. When he would grab my hand to help me over a log or across a mud hole, it was like putting your hand inside the pocket of a baseball mitt, just not as soft. He was tall, with rugged features, his skin weathered by the sun and his spirit weakened by years of hard work with little to show for it. He wore bib overalls, the denim fabric long ago devoid of color, just a muted blue, like the wild morning glory flowers that grew mixed in among the mushmelons at the edge of the tobacco fields. Mushmelons look like miniature watermelons, the round "Sugar Baby" kind. What a joy it was to stomp a mushmelon and hear the resulting pop!

Grandaddy, Daddy, Uncle Paul, and I had climbed into Daddy's old '51 Ford automobile. It was hot and dry, the dog days of summer as Grandma called it, most likely mid-July, I think. We were on the Dixie Bridge Road and Grandaddy was saying if it didn't rain soon the tobacco crop was really going to be in danger of not "making." Tobacco has a lot of "come out" in it, as he always phrased it, but if we don't get a good soaking rain in the next few weeks, it may be too late for it to come out.

I could tell the tone was serious. There was not the usual laughter on this ride, but its significance for the time being was lost on me. Daddy's '51 Ford had been an old Police Interceptor; it had a 289 V-8 engine with a three-speed on the column shifter, and it would fly! Today, however, the old Ford crept slowly along, barely twenty miles per hour, a choking red dust cloud roiled in its wake. Along the road's edge the cow itch, poison sumac, and honeysuckle vines clinging tight to the time-worn cedar fenceposts were wilted and drooped in the afternoon sun, and coated in a thick layer of dust, the residue from the passing of prior vehicles.

Out in the pastures even the cattle were not immune; the white Charolais beef cattle that belonged to Melvin Gill were tinged in a surreal tone of the red Virginia clay. Melvin Gill owned all the land on both sides of the Dixie Bridge Road, as well as the cattle in the pastures for miles in each direction. Someone intoned,

"This is a lot of land and cattle, ain't it," and it seemed to strike a chord with Grandaddy.

I was only five years old but I was going to start school that year. School would start just ahead of my birthday on September 7, but we had received a letter in the mail saying I would be allowed to go instead of having to wait till the next year. I was excited in some ways and yet anxious in others. Grandaddy had taught me to count to a hundred using acorns down at the barn. I could say my ABCs backwards and forwards and even read some simple words from the cartoons in the *Progressive Farmer* magazines we received.

"Jimmy, there's somethin' you need to know," Grandaddy said.

He began to tell me of how kids had picked on him when he was in school because he had patches sewn over spots where holes had worn in his clothes, and because all he had for lunch were butter-and-jelly biscuits he took in a paper tote sack.

"Same thing probably happen to you," he said.

Daddy and Uncle Paul recounted similar stories.

"Why is that?" I asked.

He paused and said, "Well there's different kinds of folks in the world, po folks, middle folks, and rich folks. We are just po folks."

I had never known we were "po folks" and to be honest I didn't know what it meant. All I knew was that now school didn't seem like so much fun and I said, "I don't think I'll go to school then."

For the first time they all laughed and said, "You ain't got no choice; the state makes you do it."

The rest of the ride was just a blur, as I sat there on the front seat between them, Daddy and Grandaddy. In my mind's eye I saw all the bad things that were waiting for me when I went to school. I had always thought out the way things would be before they happened, and worried over them. Grandma had told me more than once, "You got too much imagination for your own good."

We got home, and I hit the woods. It was the one place where I was the most comfortable. It was not unusual for me to walk for miles in the surrounding hardwoods and bottomland swamps behind the house. I knew where the deer bedded, where the turkeys roosted, where the bobwhite coveys were likely to be at any time during the day and where two springs on opposite ends of my range bubbled ice-cold water from far beneath the surface. I would stop at them the most often and bend down for long cold drinks of the sweetest water you can imagine. The trees here were old, thick canopy hardwoods, and there was little undergrowth so you had a wide range of vision in any direction. I would sit on the high hillside above the spring, serenaded by summer insects, and it was not unusual to see deer, smaller animals, and birds come and enjoy the cold, clear water below. I could imagine Indians in years past, living here high on this knoll, and hunting the game-rich hills and swamps. I spent many afternoons here myself, stalking imaginary buffalo, with a bow made from a sweet gum branch, bent and tied with tobacco twine, and stickweeds for arrows.

This "po folks" thing had me spooked and I needed more information; I knew where to get it too! She was standing over the woodstove, waist-length hair tightly wound in a bun, wire rim glasses, an old, faded print dress she had made years ago, and a worn-out old apron. Grandma was a small woman with small hands, but they were not that wrinkled or calloused for her age. I guess it was the Jergens lotion she always seemed to be rubbing on them.

Uncle Page had killed a chicken the day before; I had come around the corner of the house just in time to see it spinning, wings flapping, rolling over and over until the nerves ran out of oxygen, and it was still, forever more. The head was picked up and flung into the wood line. The body was submerged in hot water; the feathers plucked; and the chicken gutted and cleaned. The memory of all that was quickly subdued by the sweet smell and tantalizing sizzle of fried chicken in the cast-iron pan on the woodstove.

As you entered the small kitchen there was a water bucket and dipper sitting on a small handmade wood table, covered in a faded pink linen cloth, flanked to the left by a dented aluminum wash pan and a bar of Octagon soap. An old refrigerator loudly whirred and hummed just in front of them and on the left wall. On the right wall was the woodbox, chock full of split firewood, crumpled newspaper, and lightwood kindling for the woodstove. In the center of the room, under a 40-watt bulb hanging as if by a thread from some thin electrical wire, six mismatched chairs surrounded the table, covered with a faded red-and-white checkerboard oilcloth. Against the far wall was an old white china cabinet, trimmed in green and filled with dishes Grandma had gotten from the boxes of Quaker Oatmeal she never failed to buy weekly. All our glassware was oatmeal glass; Quaker Oatmeal put a glass, cup, saucer, something in every round box, and Grandma loved her oatmeal. That glasses had a stamped pattern of crosses and stars and were in a transparent color that seemed to not know if it was light gray or light green.

I just sat down at the table. Didn't say a word, didn't have to. Grandma knew that if I was sitting still ever, something was wrong.

"What you so happy a boat?" she asked.

I hemmed and hawed and eventually told her about the car ride and what the men folks had said. I then told her I didn't want to go to school and why. She did a very strange thing: we hadn't had supper yet but she cut a small slice of the "Raggedy" coconut pie, as I called it, that she had made. She made her own pie crust and they were always moist and flaky. The top was a thick layer of long strands of freshly grated coconut; sandwiched in the middle was a rich custard of fresh eggs, vanilla extract, coconut milk, and sugar. It was hard to get high heat in the oven of the woodstove, so the pies were never dry, always bursting with moisture and goodness.

"Eat this," she said.

Strange thing or not, I didn't question this opportunity. I finished it and slid the saucer aside.

"That pie," she said, "got a bottom crust, a middle, and a top crust. You might be the bottom crust but it don't matter; you got to have it all or it ain't pie, and everybody likes pie."

I wasn't sure I understood much better than before, but my mind had been taken away from whatever the root cause of my concern had been. She was right; everybody did like pie, and as I walked away from the table, and out of the kitchen I thought to myself, *I like the middle of the pie best; the middle, that's what I want to be.* I didn't know it at the time, but I guess on some subconscious level I had just set a goal.

High Cost of Meat

One of my first real memories, the kind that stick to you like the red clay mud of southeastern Virginia, was of a chilly, early November morning. We had gone through several killing frosts, the kind where the dead brown grass and outbuildings look like they are encrusted in diamonds and your every breath forms a fog. We had no indoor plumbing and the winter visits to an outhouse somehow curtail the "need to go"; if you went, you really needed to go!

Southeastern Virginia and South Hill in particular have a dialect that is so distinct you can recognize it anywhere, anytime. Even now, fifty years removed, people either know where I'm from or ask where I'm from. It is a brogue similar to the Outer Banks area of North Carolina. Probably a result of being some of the oldest European inhabited land in North America.

O*at*, not *out*; *doeg*, not *dog*; *hoese*, not *house*; and *hoeg*, not *hog*, and we had two. Hogs, that is.

I remember when we got them. Grandma called them "feeder pigs," which meant they had been weaned from the mother and were old enough to eat solid food hence the "feeder" label. Cute as any puppy and just as much fun. I liked to feed them, mostly table scraps since we could not afford food, even if it had been available.

"Go slop the hogs" was the command.

"Feed 'em and forget 'em," Grandma would always say.

Why, I wondered, *when they were so much fun?*

Over the course of the summer they became no longer just hogs; they became "Dixie" and "Rat." A sow and a boar of a breed Grandma called "Land Raisers," long, off-white, with coarse hair, and very muscular. Unfortunately, muscular is just another word for "meaty."

My Uncle Page was a man's man. Decorated twice in World War II with the Purple Heart for wounds in combat. He chewed tobacco, said what he meant and meant what he said, would not back away from a fight, took crap from no one, and did all things unspeakable. If you needed a pig or bull castrated, he did it. No charge. I say "no charge" but just give him the testicles; he ate them! "Bull fries" they called them if beef, "mountain oysters" if pork. He also killed and butchered pretty much everyone's animals in the area. Payment was usually a piece of meat.

He had come by the night before, and there had seemed to be some type excitement about what was to happen the next day. I remember them talking about scalding water, getting the spices needed to make sausage, and everyone seemed upbeat. A rare occurrence in my world.

I was awakened really early, about five a.m., by rustling and voices in the kitchen. I might have been five going on six but I was drinking coffee like everyone else. Uncle Page was in the kitchen and I had coffee and fatback biscuits with Grandaddy, Grandma, and Uncle Page.

My Uncle Bo, who also lived there, came in and said, "The water is boiling and ready."

Uncle Page said, "We might as well do it then."

And they headed to the pig pen. I followed along behind. Uncle Page took his .22 rifle and a big, long butcher knife. I didn't know why, but I was getting a sick feeling in my stomach as we walked down to the pen in the light of a kerosene lantern. Uncle Bo put some slop in the feed trough and Rat came over to eat. Uncle Page raised the rifle and shot Rat between the eyes, just above the nose. He squealed and dropped to his front knees. My mind was screaming — what? and why? — but my lips couldn't form any words. Then Uncle Page drove the big knife between Rat's front legs just under the chin, and blood squirted all over his shoes and pants. Rat rolled on his side and as his heart pumped, blood continued to shoot in spurts.

Dixie cowered at the back of the pen; nothing would coax her forward and I knew that somehow, she knew as well. Uncle Bo kicked the pen boards down with his foot, Uncle Page swung over and shot, but the bullet hit Dixie in the nose only. She squealed, an ungodly, otherworldly squeal, but mercifully the second shot dropped her to her knees. Again the knife, again the blood.

I hated this, I hated it all. … I just stumbled off and sat down.

They put the hogs in the scalding water and scraped the hair off with jar lids and then hung them up and gutted them. Nothing was wasted. The intestines were cleaned. Liver, lungs, all saved. The fat was cooked down into liquid, which when cooled formed lard, and the skin or "cracklings" would be used in cornbread. Feet, ears, tails, the meat from the head and cheeks were boiled into a gelatin and chopped and cooked into souse meat. Brains were saved to be cooked with eggs for breakfast. All scrap lean and fat were mixed with pepper and sage and ground into sausage by a local store for a charge of seven cents per pound.

Those that helped took a shoulder … I took a memory.

The high cost of meat is much more than a metaphor for money. I don't remember ever eating any of Dixie and Rat but the next year my Grandma's words rang true: "feed 'em and forget 'em" had an all-new meaning.

After that I avoided hog killings at all costs, except those that still happen at night. Even now, I will sometimes awaken, in a cold drenching sweat, as I hear the scream that Dixie made, and I knew that she knew.

RECIPE: Cracklings

The skin that was removed from the hogs, with the fat attached to it, was cut into long, roughly 3/4-inch-wide strips, then cut into pieces about the size of a man's thumb. These were placed into a large cast-iron pot with about an inch of oil in the bottom of the pot, to keep everything from sticking. The pot was placed over a white-hot wood fire and the contents were carefully stirred. If the oil started to smoke, it was too hot and in danger of burning. Coals would be raked quickly aside, then added back slowly.

As it cooks, fat is rendered from the skin and turns into oil, which is then allowed to cool. As it cools, the oil turns into lard, a white natural shortening or grease. Lard was stored in big metal tins and used in everything from biscuits and pie crusts right on down to being the grease used to coat the inside of wagon wheels.

As they cook, the skins brown and rise to the top and are then scooped off. These leftover skins are the cracklings, most likely named for the sound they make when you bite them.

Cracklings will usually keep for months at room temperature.

A favorite of mine, especially when covered in homemade melted butter, was Cracklin' Corn Bread.

RECIPE: Grandma's Cracklin' Corn Bread

Remove the tough skins of the cracklins with a knife and save for dog treats. In the cornbread just use the crisp fat and small traces of lean beneath the skin.

2 cups stone-ground cornmeal
1 1/2 teaspoons salt
1 tablespoon baking powder
2 "cups" buttermilk; Grandma measured by small coffee cups so I'm going to say 1 standard cup of buttermilk
2 "cups" cracklins; again, most likely 1 standard cup of cracklins

Mix the cornmeal and the salt. Cut in the baking powder, buttermilk and stir.
Add in the cracklins and mix yet again.
If it looks a little dry, add just a touch of warm water.

Bake in the woodstove or oven at about 350 degrees until the top browns.

I liked to cut the cornbread in half, add butter (till Grandma took it away from me) and then load it down with turnip greens, vinegar, and salt, making a sandwich.

RECIPE: Grandma's Apple Betty

Sometimes just the simplest recipes are best. Such was the case with apple betty.

Mrs. Baisey had a crab apple tree, which had been on the property when they bought it. They did not use the apples, and Grandma, never one for "lettin' things go to waste," would go over there when they started ripening and falling off the tree. Grandma, who almost always had her apron on, would just pick up ripe apples under the tree and put them in her apron, which she held by the corners with her left hand. Usually she just got enough for maybe two "fixins," as she called them. She would give Mrs. Baisey eggs from time to time when we had more than we needed, and Mrs. Baisey gave her crab apples and damsons.

Grandma would make a few extra biscuits for breakfast and then crumble them up into small fine crumbles.

She would peel the apples and thinly slice them inward toward the core but leaving the cores intact, these she would just toss into the bucket for the hogs. She usually ended up with about 4 cups of apple slices. Her "cups," however, were just the small coffee cups we drank out of, not a "measuring cup." I don't know what amount they held but it was not a lot; they were less than half the size of the typical coffee mugs we use today.

She took a patty of homemade butter and generously rubbed a baking dish; if a few small chunks broke off in the process you just left them in there.

Then she took about 1/2 cup of brown sugar and sprinkled it on the sides and the bottom of the dish, along with a few shots of ground cinnamon.

On top of the sugar she put about a third of the apples and sprinkled about a third of the crumbled biscuits on them.

Then another 1/2 cup of brown sugar sprinkled in and a few shots of ground cinnamon.

Another layer of apples, and another layer of biscuit crumbs on top of them.

Add another 1/2 cup of brown sugar, a shot or two of cinnamon, and the rest of the apples.

Add the rest of the crumbled biscuits to cover the apples and form the top layer.

Then she would cut a chunk out of the butter patty, about the width of a butter stick, and start slicing it about 1/8 inch thick and covering the whole top of the bread crumbs with butter slices.

She generously sprinkled a little brown sugar and cinnamon on top of the butter.

She would put about 4 or 5 tablespoons of water in a bowl and sprinkle it, like a baptism with her fingers, all across the top.

She covered the pan with a piece of aluminum foil, which she always just saved and used over and over until it fell apart.

The betty baked at 375 degrees for about 45 minutes to an hour, in the woodstove.

You take the foil off during the last 5 minutes or so; the top will brown and the apples, sugar, and butter should be just bubbling in the dish.

You had to be careful about the last serving in the bowl. Everyone would say they "were full" and didn't want it, but when you reached for it, you could end up with a fork in your hand.

School Ain't So Bad

It was my first day of school. I was nervous, so nervous in fact, I had cut myself shaving that morning … kidding, of course … but I was "fidgety." I had a cup of coffee and a fatback biscuit, but not seconds and thirds as usual. Grandma had made sure I started off in the cleanest, pressed, hand-me-down clothing I had. She checked to see that my ears and hands were scrubbed, fingernails clipped, and freshly cut hair slicked down. I was GQ material!

He was my second cousin, but the first time I remember seeing him, someone called him Uncle Clyde, so that's what I called him. Clyde Thompson or Uncle Clyde drove Bus 3, and little did I know when I stepped on it that first morning I was beginning a tradition that would span twelve years, with the last being by far the longest.

Bus 3 was the newest in the fleet, but all I knew was that when it showed up in our driveway it was long and it was big! As I stepped on the bus Uncle Clyde said, "Morning, Jimmy," in a tone so loud everyone could hear it. I immediately felt important. I also immediately felt conspicuous. The bus looked like a hallway without end, and it was over half full. Suddenly it was now quiet as a tomb, and all eyes looking my way. There was an open seat directly behind him and I jumped on it.

Uncle Clyde was a big man, balding with short-cropped gray hair on each side, and horn-rimmed spectacles. He was usually smiling, but from time to time when we would get rowdy, he would stop the bus and give us "what's for."

The ride to school was fun, actually; I got to see where other kids lived and the atmosphere on the ride was jovial.

I was in Mrs. Ellington's class. Mrs. Paulette, the school secretary, helped me find my room, and we settled in. I remember Mrs. Ellington as somewhat thin, tall with shoulder-length gray hair and as always smiling, always a pleasant disposition. I liked the feeling I would get when she said "Very good", or "Well done" and I would always try to do my best when called upon because of this.

The classroom was a small square with one whole wall of large paned windows, which could be opened or closed, facing the street, and small wooden desks, which we would push against the wall at naptime. At the back of the room was the "cloak room" and bathroom. The bathroom was tiny, with a miniature toilet and thick wooden door, and although I didn't like to use it at the time, it would turn out to be much nicer than using the big communal "Boys' Room," since that's where all the school fights tended to occur.

Mrs. Ellington said she needed to know what we already knew, so we started off counting to ten I think, and it was a breeze since I could already go to 100. Then on to the ABCs, also fun and also easy. We were given a "milk break" each morning and although I hated milk, I found chocolate milk to be not that bad and actually came to like it. Reading also came pretty naturally and the "See Dick run," See Spot play," "Run, Sally, run" pages became routine pretty quickly.

Lunchtime came and I took my bag of peanut butter and jelly sandwiches to the cafeteria and bought a chocolate milk, which I think cost four cents. No one teased or said anything. My attention, however, was focused on the meal on the lunch trays. They looked and smelled like a wish you'd get after rubbing Aladdin's lamp. I didn't know then what it was. It was baked spaghetti and meat sauce, made of ground beef and cheese. Cheese I knew, rat cheese anyway, but this was different and ground beef was a new one to me. I had never heard of it or had it as far as I knew. Someone said it was kinda like a meatball. The closest smell I could associate with it was the Chef-Boy-are-Dee and cheese spaghetti in a can we sometimes had, and getting a meatball was rare, you might get a small piece of one but never a whole one. The smell of freshly baked yeast rolls permeated the air, and they had vanilla fudge twirl ice cream in little cups with wooden ice cream spoons, the first time I'd seen it as well, and I had to ask what it was.

A few days later I was informed if I wanted to "work" in the cafeteria I could get school lunch. It was a dream come true! I asked at home and Daddy said it was okay but probably better if I didn't tell anyone … made no sense to me. Again, I felt important; I had a job in the cafeteria! At ten minutes before lunch Mrs. Ellington would say, "Jimmy, you may be excused"; that was the cue we had agreed on. It simply meant go to the cafeteria to help out. It was a short trip down the wide hall and past the school trophy case to the open, spacious lunchroom.

The lunch ladies were the nicest folks I had met outside of family. Come to think of it, they may have been about the only folks I had met out of family except a few at Hines Store. Mrs. Wynn or Mrs. Harris almost always gave me a fresh, hot roll straight from the oven before I started stacking the trays and silverware for everyone to eat with. As the lunch line started I was ushered to the back to clean pots or pans and as one of the ladies, I believe Miss Carpenter, said, "This way no one has to see you, and then they won't make fun." I thought it was kind that they took the time to protect me, and even though I was constantly being told to be ready for this, it had yet to happen.

After the kids ate and left, we were fed our lunch. There were usually three to five of us. Every day was a new taste sensation. I had pimento cheese sandwiches, sloppy joes, peach cobbler, and on occasion an Eskimo Pie, all things I had never had before. Recess and morning free time were fun, but lunch was my new favorite part of school. We ate and then cleared and cleaned the tables and straightened the chairs before returning to class.

After lunch we had "naptime," the most God-awful time of day for me. We all had to bring "mats" to school to sleep on. Some kids had thick comfortable mats and I just had a large towel but that wasn't the problem. The problem was I never napped at home. I would always just roam the fields hunting arrowheads, fish, or tramp around in the woods. I didn't like being confined, and again I was fidgety.

Reading came naturally to me and Mrs. Ellington said I had a pleasant voice, whatever that was, and she called on me a lot to read out loud. I liked doing that. We got our first report cards and I had gotten all A's and B's. The only marks I had against me were Attendance (two missed days due to strep throat) and Behavior (I was disruptive at naptime). I guess truly I was. I was like a dog. I would circle the mat several times, get up, move left to right, switch from head to toe, hum, I even mouth-called bobwhite at times. Everyone laughed, but not Mrs. Ellington. When I got home with the report card Grandaddy couldn't have been happier if they had been his grades and in reality they were. He had made me all I was.

Mornings at school were fantastic. Kids of all ages played a game called Prisoners' Base. There was a pole on each side of the playground separated by a painted line. You formed a team on each side of the line and chose teammates. If your team could run in a complete circle around the pole on the other side without being "tagged," you received a point. If tagged, you became a prisoner. The first prisoner held the pole with one hand and extended the other hand horizontally. If another was tagged, he held the hand of the first prisoner and extended his hand. Girls and boys played, and I liked holding the hand of a girl; I didn't want to be "freed." If you could touch the extended hand of the prisoner without being tagged yourself, they were all freed. Any that were tagged before they could cross the line back to their side were prisoners again. You got a point for each prisoner freed.

This was a game made for me. I had very fast bursts of speed and was agile in dodging opponents, a result of dodging trees while running full bore through the woods. Although it was mainly older kids playing, I was always one of the first teammates chosen, and by midyear I became the "captain," the person on each side who picked the team.

I wore the sliding board, merry-go-round, and monkey bars out!

The boys would team up, with a big kid on the bottom and a little kid on his shoulders, and "chicken fight," again a game tailor-made for me. I had no mercy, and we were seldom beaten, my partner and I.

First grade came and went in a blur. Near the end we took our class picture. I had forgotten to take the information home, or most likely had simply made a "paper plane" with it and sent it on its way through the bus window. At any rate, when we took pictures, I had worn the same clothes to school as I had the day before, and had not combed my hair at all. Grandma, being busy, had "missed" nabbing me before I boarded the bus. She was mortified when she saw it, and said, "You look like an orphan in that thing." To me it looked no different than what I saw in the mirror every day. I did notice I had a "set of ears" hung on me, and I would hear that from quite a few others in the coming years, but ignorance is bliss.

Reflecting back on the last few weeks of school, I realized I had not been teased, had maintained good grades, and had even learned to nap, albeit fitfully and very briefly.

It was almost June and the end of the school year. Someone in the second grade where we were headed told us we would learn "cursive" writing the next year, and how difficult that was. According to him only two kids were passing the whole second grade out of three whole classes, less than one kid per class, and I bought it hook, line, and sinker. I got home that afternoon and told Grandaddy what was said. He assured me "twont right" and said not to worry; I would know "cursive" before the summer was over and be a step ahead next year.

The weight of school had been removed and I knew that as long as I had Grandaddy I had nothing to worry about. By the grace of God, that was all that I knew.

Teachers

There are people who touch lives, in a way they never know
Gentle souls in walks of life, where fame will seldom go
Often quiet, unpretentious, start a seed that needs to grow
Like a fragrance in the breeze, short lived, and yet loved so
Paint a picture on a canvas, that stands the test of time
Might be no more than a thought, somehow touching a child's mind
Maybe only just a prod, a simple nudge, and nothing more
Ignite a memory that helps them suffer, a loss, a death, a war
With their words they mold a life, a foundation for the soul
From the cradle to the grave, shared alike by young and old
Somehow springing from the past, a memory shared so long ago
Meant nothing at the moment, but now more than you could know
Shared our childhood at a time, when when no one could really reach us
But their kindness lasts forever, as does the memory of those teachers
What they give us can't be bought or sold, in truth it can't be measured
Knowledge gained worth more than gold, or any earthly

treasure
The time we shared was brief, like a snowflake in the wind
Impact on our lives eternal, not just a teacher, but a friend
If you made it your life's work, know that we all, truly care
You may never hear the thank you, but please know that
it's there
And I hope we somehow gave you, small pieces of our
heart
It was all we had to spare, but somehow it's a start
And with our words and deeds, we will praise you from
afar
For it was you and you alone, that made us what we are

Common Bullies

Just this year I have become reacquainted with an old schoolmate who has moved back to South Hill. We were friends in school, but not really close friends, since in some ways we were from two different worlds. My friend — now we truly are friends — and I were talking. It turns out that alcohol in the homeplace and schoolyard bullies were the two problems he struggled with as much as I did. I was really shocked when I learned they were the same bullies that plagued me. Bullies like alcohol show no deference!

Alcohol was almost an accepted fact among folks in Southside Virginia. It ran the gamut. It discriminated against no one, poor, middle-class, rich; it was there for all of us. Abject poverty, middle-class blues, rich anxiety, it all needs to be alleviated.

As far as my situation, it probably robbed us of some better clothes, maybe a proper diet, but it was for my Daddy a needed outlet.

Beer

As far back as I can remember, Daddy was drinking beer. I remember Krueger, Schaeffer, Rheingold, Old Milwaukee. Some were as low as sixty-nine cents a six-pack. No pop tops then. You had to have what was sarcastically called a "church key," or can opener, to get in them.

My early memories of alcohol were not bad ones though. Daddy, Grandaddy, Uncle Bob, Uncle Paul, and I would pile in Daddy's old '51 Ford and take off to go riding in what is still my favorite spot in the area. The Dixie's Bridge Road.

The mood in the car would always be a happy one. Happiness was something I seemed to see only on Sundays, and even at four or five years old I associated happiness with beer. If only they would let me have one!

We would always stop, and I would walk out on the bridge. The men for whatever reason always walked just off the road, into the edge of the woods, and seemed to stand there looking at something. I guess they never found it because they would all turn around and come back to the car at about the same time. Eventually it dawned on me: this was a bathroom break!

We would ride and look at other folks' tobacco crops and discuss how bad or good they looked. Usually we would stop for another six-pack, often at Badeye's store. It was illegal to sell beer on Sunday, but we would park under the huge pin oak tree up front, and Daddy and I would walk to the back door. Somehow knowing that what we were doing was wrong only made it that much better.

The store was closed; Badeye would come to the door and let us in. Mr. McKinley was his real name; he wore a black eye patch and everyone called him "Badeye." He seemed resigned to the moniker and no one ever asked, as far as I know, how he lost the eye.

Mr.and Mrs. McKinley could not have children. But they had a black Chihuahua mix named Trusty, and they introduced him to everyone as their son. He was extremely intelligent and had an extensive repertoire of tricks. My favorite was when they dressed him up as a cowboy in a little outfit she had sewed for him, complete with a gun belt with two pistols and a cowboy hat, and he would walk upright on two legs.

I would pet Trusty as a fresh, cold six-pack and a few pieces of penny candy or cookies were put in the brown paper bag. Uncle Paul would take the bag once the beer was gone and blow it up like a balloon and pop it. He could make it sound as loud as any gunshot.

Saturday nights they all went to Claude Daniels's and drank a few cold beers. Claude Daniels's was a simple one-room store with three short aisles of canned goods facing you as you walked in. As you turned right you walked over to a long Formica-topped bar with the cash register in the middle. To the right was a glass display case from which he sold "Saturday Night Specials" — cheap pistols, usually $19.95 to $39.95 and either .22, .25, or .32 in caliber. No license check, you just had to be eighteen or he had to know you. He sold pickled eggs, hoop cheese, pickled pigs' feet, and oil sausage, but the main attraction was ice-cold beer for fifty cents a can. It was a very socially mixed crowd. I would hear the last name of someone who had the same last name as a classmate and was surprised to find out that it was his or her dad.

At Claude Daniels's store the rich and poor mingled freely, and the mood was always jovial. It had to be the beer! When they left, they would always bring home penny candy again, while we, the women and kids, struggled to make out a picture on Grandma's old black-and-white TV. I remember *Saturday Night at the Movies*, *Mission: Impossible*, or *The Man from U.N.C.L.E.* playing. You didn't have to wonder what was on the other three channels because we got just the one.

After Grandaddy died, Daddy's mood when he was drinking was no longer a happy one. He would brood and talk of things in life he was unhappy with, and on occasion even threaten suicide. One Sunday he and Momma had gone for a ride. Hours passed and they did not return. I was looking down the dirt road and there came Momma alone, walking. I ran out, and Grandma followed slowly behind me.

"The car broke down, your Daddy's said he's gonna set it on fire and then climb back in it," she said.

I was terrified. I could see the car, a blazing inferno with

Daddy trapped inside. It could all be over by now, I thought.

Grandma looked at me and said, "Jimmy, your Daddy ain't gonna burn that car."

Uncle Page happened to drive up, and after a brief repeat of the story he told me to "hop in." We found Daddy and the car exactly where Momma had said, on the old Powell Place road. He was just sitting inside it, calmly drinking a beer. Uncle Page figured out what was wrong, they fixed the car, and he drove it home.

Daddy began to get home later and later, and I always sat on the couch at Grandma's looking out the window every five minutes, checking for headlights.

"He ain't been in no wreck, he's just up at Claude Daniels's," she would say.

One hot summer night he left about half a can of Old Milwaukee on the front porch by his wooden chair. He went in and went to bed and I decided it was time to see what beer was like. I had long anticipated the chance to have one, and I knew this was going to be great! It was one of the biggest letdowns I had encountered in my few years of life. God, was that an awful taste; how can they drink this, I wondered. It was like another childhood dream had been shattered. Santa Claus and now this.

I told Grandma I was sick of being around beer and that I would never drink the stuff. But as my later teenage years came, I found myself doing just that. She never said anything, but one night maybe ten years later, I had come up for a visit. Daddy and I had gone for a ride down Dixie's Bridge Road and drank a six-pack. I had taken him home and gone back to Grandma's house. She had some homemade potato soup, navy beans, and tater cakes left over from supper. Whenever she made mashed potatoes at lunch she would save what was left over, pat it out into little pancakes at night, and fry them in the cast-iron pan. It was a meal to die for.

As I sat quietly eating, she came to the kitchen table, sat down with a cup of coffee, calmly looked at me, took a slow sip, and said, "You told me you were never gonna do that."

She said nothing else, just sat there. Knowing that I had disappointed her was like a dagger through the heart. She could communicate the strongest message in the gentlest manner that to this day I have ever seen. Even now, thirty years later, I will find myself sitting at a hotel bar after a business meeting, drinking beer with a friend, and out of nowhere a wave of shame will wash over me. And I know when I feel it, it's her; she hasn't given up on me. "You told me you were never gonna do that." I can see her face, and I can hear her voice. And I always then push the beer away. Half full, full, it doesn't matter. I say goodnight and walk on off to bed.

FROSTY MUG

Staring at a frosty mug, wondering what's the pull?
Give up your kids, your wife, your land
Just to keep it full.
Spend your life reflecting, on what might have been,
Had you just resisted drinking that first can.

It didn't even taste good, made you sick as hell
But like some real good water, you go back to the well.
It's one, it's two, it's three, it's four, a six-pack a night.
Seems like it's always taking more, to get to feeling right.

Cause a beer can makes me happy, wine glass makes me
cry, liquor makes me sick as hell, but somehow I'll get by,
Lord, somehow I'll get by.

Wife tried to slow you down, all to no avail
Boss man did the same, told him, you go straight to hell.
Now you're doing shooters, shot of liquor and a beer.
Fought a man twice my size tonight; a drunk man has no fear.

Face in the mirror gets older every day.
Don't many folks come by the house, even old friends stay away.
Somehow it just don't matter, don't make a damn to me.
Got cold beer in the cooler, that's all I really need.

Cause a beer can makes me happy, wine glass makes me

cry, liquor makes me sick as hell, but somehow I'll get by,
Lord, somehow I'll get by.

Now I'm only 55, doctor says you're dead, if you don't
stop drinking,
Better get that through your head.

A lifetime of memories flashing through my mind,
sitting in the doorway sipping on some wine,
Waiting on my neighbor to get back from the store,
I ran out of liquor, had to get some more.

I woke up this morning, couldn't lift my head;
eyeballs was yellow, not the usual red.
I know my days is over, wish I knew where I'd been;
I'd love to start over, do it all again.

If I owned up to it, and for once was a man,
I'd admit I often wished I'd never picked up that first can.
Beer can makes me happy, wine glass makes me cry, liquor
makes me sick as hell, but now it's time to die, Lord, now
it's time to die.

The Lazy Days Of Summer

It was an unusually warm Sunday for mid September. Uncle Bob and Daddy were setting on the front porch at Grandma's and had been laughing and talking about going up to Buggs Island, and going swimming, seeing as how it was so hot.

Buggs Island is what the local folks call the John H. Kerr Dam and Reservoir.

"I tell you what," Uncle Bob said. "The rod is in the car; let's go up to the Nottoway River and see if we can't catch some catfish."

"Fine with me," Daddy said; "we'll stop by Badeye's and get a little bait."

They both laughed aloud at that one.

"Jimmy, go dig some red wigglers," Uncle Bob said.

I grabbed the pitchfork and went to the mule shed. Grandaddy would always take any worms left when they bought red wigglers and dump them under a little dirt at the back of the mule shed. The manure back there over the years had mixed with the sandy, loamy soil to form a rich black earth as fertile as any potting soil. It was easy to dig in and every pitchfork full turned up almost as many fat wriggling worms as it did dirt.

I had a Banner Breakfast Sausage can filled in no time. As I walked back to the house I thought to myself, *I'd rather eat these worms than what was originally in this can.* I don't know what was in Banner Breakfast Sausage but I had long suspected it must be pork brains, because to me it had a taste that was a cross between fried pork brains and the taste of the lead on the fishing line when you put it in your mouth and bit down on it to make it stay tight on the line. I shuddered and walked on to the house.

We loaded Daddy's old black Ford, Uncle Bob riding shotgun and me in back, knees tucked under and sitting on my feet so I could see outside the car. We pulled under the tree at Badeye's. As Daddy and I got out, Uncle Bob pulled out a dollar and said, "Here, I got the beer. We're burning your gas."

I don't care how many times we did it, somehow the walk to

the back door of the closed store on Sunday to get something you wasn't supposed to be able to buy was just always special. We tapped and "Mrs. Mac" as Daddy called Mrs. McKinley opened the door.

"Where's Badeye?" Daddy asked.

"He's under the weather today; we didn't even go to church yesterday." Mr. and Mrs. McKinley were Catholic and they went to something they called "Mass" on Saturdays.

"Can I get a six-pack of Krueger," Daddy said, "and a pack of Winstons? Might as well let the chap get a few penny cookies too," he said.

"Don't worry about the cookies, I got something for Jimmy," she said. She wiped her hands on her apron and went off into the back of the store to her kitchen. She came back with three fat, big old round sugar cookies with colored sprinkles on them.

"Thank you, Mrs. McKinley," I said.

As we walked out the back door into the sun and on to the car, we both carried a treasure in two separate sacks.

"Church key in the glove box, Bob," Daddy said as he backed out.

Yep, I thought. Church key in the glove box, the trunk, Daddy's tackle box, and the old metal tackle box I had found in the shed and laid claim to. The church key in my box was so rusty though it would probably have given them lockjaw.

South Hill was "Sunday morning quiet"; hardly any traffic out at all. As we went by the big brick Methodist Church across from Boney Hudson's station, I saw little girls in brightly colored church dresses frolicking on the front lawn, as the old women with their blue, curly hair chatted among themselves. The men in their Sunday suits were standing in groups smoking cigarettes and laughing.

As we went by Crews Funeral Home, Uncle Bob said, "They must have a body; Bobby Crews's car is over there."

We turned right just above the Colonial Theatre. I had never been there but was looking forward to one day seeing a movie. I had heard Uncle Paul say the screen was "bout as big as y'all's whole house."

We rode on out of town, by Madam Eden the "Fortune Teller's" house. The thought of someone knowing your future was scary enough by itself; I had never wanted to go there.

Next up was Simmons Terminal, the truck stop. Daddy had worked there a while until a big metal restrainer that you put around the center of the tire when blowing it up had expanded too far and exploded. Another few inches and he would have been killed, he said; he had quit after that.

Simmons had an unnamed barbershop sitting in a tiny little side room, barely big enough for four people to fit in. The door was open, so Uncle Johnny was there, a gray-haired, pencil-thin black man who always had a lit cigarette, which he rolled himself, dangling from the corner of his mouth. He never took it out except to light another one with it. The ashes just fell off by themselves as it bobbed up and down while he laughed and talked. He cut hair and shined shoes. I liked going there; he would tease and joke and ask questions about school and fishing and such. I often got my hair cut there for a dollar.

In that day and time everyone, white or black — and it didn't matter which color they were — if he or she was older than you, they were respectfully called "Uncle" or "Aunt." Each and every time I addressed them, right on up until they passed away, I called them Uncle or Aunt, as I still do to those still alive. It was a simple, time-honored courtesy that was part of the family heritage of most folks in Southside Virginia, and it continues to be in generations still being raised.

Out past Park View High School. And Wayside Park, a little turnout facing some beautiful old-growth hardwoods and stocked with two or three picnic tables. On up to Big Fork. Here Highway 1 continued on to the Roanoke River. If you turned right, you went up to Buggs Island Lake and the Rock Quarry. We kept straight, past the South Hill Motel. The rooms looked about half full and the restaurant staff was beginning to get ready for the after-church lunch crowd.

"Oh hell," Daddy said and braked quickly into the motel parking lot. "Ain't nowhere to get a beer up Number 1," he said.

We turned and headed for Buggs Island. It took about four times asking but I finally got him to agree to take me to the Rock Quarry. All the rock for the construction of the big dam, which had created Buggs Island Lake, had come from here and the resulting hole was huge. Probably an eighth of a mile across and hundreds and hundreds of feet deep. We drove the short, weed-choked dirt road down to the quarry. The quarry was closed by just a barbed wire fence and nothing else. Its sides were a beautiful blue-gray granite, and it was filled with cobalt blue water. The sheer rock walls looked straight down, but you could throw a rock with all your might and you would never see it hit the water. Most times it didn't. It was an optical illusion; the walls really went out and not in.

There was an old abandoned shed at the far end, sticking out in the water, its tin roof showing but all else covered by water. Holes peppered the roof. Daddy and Uncle Bob keyed a beer and I threw rocks at the shed. "BBbbbooooom." It sounded like a shotgun blast. I had hit the tin roof and the rock went clean through the roof, echoing several times around the quarry. If you drove down to the bottom you could holler and your voice would echo back and forth two or three times.

We packed up and headed toward the dam. On the left just before you got there was a store. I never knew its name, only that it had a big sign out front that said "Last Dam Stop." It was the last station before the dam. I wasn't allowed to cuss, but I could read the sign aloud and it felt like cussing.

Uncle Bob knew the man who owned this store. He put a six-pack of Krueger and a cup of chicken livers in a bag ... better not tell Grandma about them ... and then tucked it all in a small box so no one would know what it was, and we left. I wanted to go see the dam, but Uncle Bob said we didn't have time to do that and fish too. We went back toward the rock quarry and Daddy took us on a short cut that brought us out on Highway 1 just below the river, downstream from the dam.

The Roanoke is a much wider, deeper, and prettier river than the Meherrin. Its waters were a semi-clear steel blue. We crossed over the big, arched steel bridge and drove about a half mile to an old logging road that looked like it went straight up in the air on the side of the hill. The old car sashayed left and right in the mud, but it made the climb. We parked and walked the half mile or so downhill to the river.

I was using one of Daddy's old rods. I didn't like to catfish, or river fish for that matter; you didn't get as many bites. I had no cork so I had to bottom fish. Uncle Bob and Daddy quickly caught about three catfish each. I had no luck at all.

Uncle Bob had a yellow spinner bait called a rooster tail. I asked if I could use it, and he said, "OK, but you better not lose it."

I tied it in a fisherman's knot and just to make sure, tied an extra cinch knot. After about ten casts and no luck, out of sheer boredom I put a worm on the treble hook back of the lure. As I was reeling it in, the rod almost came out of my hand. I set the hook and reeled in a big black crappie. They have a mouth almost as big as a bass; big beautiful black spotting around the throat, back, and belly; and were just a big thick slab of a fish. He was easily over a pound, and a nice addition to the stringer. In less than half a dozen casts I had caught another one.

"Remember where you caught them," Uncle Bob said. "There's probably a school of them there."

"What in the world's that noise?" Daddy asked.

I heard it too then. It was an ever-louder "bzzzzzz" like I had never heard before, like a whole herd of cicadas or "bacca flies."

"O Lawd," Uncle Bob said. "It's a bee swarm. They must have picked this as a new nesting site. Don't nobody move; we might get stung to death. If one stings, the others will smell it and might do the same."

You could see them coming across the river, almost in a big ball. Bees seemed to be everywhere I looked. There was bees in the sky, landing on the trees, rocks, the ground.

Uncle Bob said, "It's been a warm, rainy spring and summer with more flowers than usual. They likely had a good honey-producing year, so they broke off from the main hive to start a new hive. The 'Old Queen' will be with this bunch. They probably scouted this place out, and if they think you might hurt her, they will sting us."

We sat still and scared to death for close to an hour as the swarm settled and started moving over toward what looked like a big rock crevice up the hill. There were several big hollow trees there as well. Finally, Uncle Bob grabbed the fish stringer and we eased our way up and over the hill, careful where we stepped and what we touched. Somehow no one got stung at all. You could still hear them, but they didn't pay us no mind. I, for one, was glad.

We got home, took the catfish, which were now dead, and nailed their heads to an old board tacked to a sweet gum tree. Daddy cut just through the skin around the head and pulled the skin off with pliers. Uncle Bob scaled the crappie and then filleted the catfish. The crappie they just headed, gutted, and left whole.

"Better get home before I make Rachel mad," Uncle Bob said.

Daddy took a couple of catfish fillets and headed to his house. I went inside Grandma's.

"You ain't eating at my table till you wash all over; you stink to high Heaven," she said.

I spied the potato cakes, and the leftovers of a beef stew on the table. Unbeknownst to her, this would be a short bath.

TOBACCO The Golden Leaf

Today the old tobacco barns are overgrown in vines and sit sunken in, their roofs sagging like the shoulders of a worn-out old man, beaten down by the daily struggles of a hard life until he is no longer able to carry on and just tiredly sits, his head leaned down and resting on his crossed arms, waiting ever so patiently, forever slouched, and now simply resigned to his fate.

Love it or loathe it, tobacco is a beautiful crop, in my mind, from beginning to end, but tobacco defies the characterization of being classified as one's friend. Tobacco is praised for the contributions it made to the building of our great country and cursed for the myriad health issues it caused and still causes untold millions. I have smoked cigarettes almost half my life, and I still on occasion smoke cigars, but I have neither love nor hate of tobacco. For us it was simply a means to scratch a lifestyle from Virginia's hardscrabble clay as a family of sharecroppers. Today, I look back on it with great humility and a deep sense of pride, that my family had the resiliency they did to survive by growing the golden leaf.

Flue curing tobacco, without doubt, is to me one of the main sources of the pride I feel for both my family and the residents and countryside of Southside Virginia in general. It is in some ways unique to the state of Virginia, and flue curers of tobacco are genuine artisans in their own right. The particular variety goes by a variety of names: bright leaf, Virginia, or, my favorite, Gold Leaf tobacco. When done right, it is lemon or orange-yellow in color and has a heady-sweet aroma and just the mildest, sweetest taste. Whether you have an affinity for it or not, to me it was and is, the best of the best! It has a high sugar content and, ironically I guess, a low nicotine content, so it had half of what Big Tobacco wanted. It had the taste, but they would need to add more nicotine to force the addiction they were after.

60

The golden weed of Southside Virginia, though, has many redeeming qualities in the world of tobacco: it blends well with burley and Maryland tobaccos because its sugar content smooths and neutralizes the smoke. Much of this, I believe, was because of the highly labor-intensive flue curing process we used.

Flue curing involved heating the air in a half-round cement and field-rock, or solid brick, furnace that looked for all the world like the entrance to an igloo, and forcing it through large metal flues almost big enough to crawl through, into small, tight, mud-chinked log barns. There was no direct contact between the fire and the tobacco; the hot pipes or flues just heated the inside air of the curing barn, the goal being to fix or set the color on yellow and to get the desired brightness or sheen. Grandaddy would start the barn out around 90 degrees Fahrenheit and gradually over a five-day period through constant day and night monitoring and fire stoking, cure it out to around 170 degrees Fahrenheit. As tobacco yellows, the starches change to sugars at about the same rate as the color of the tobacco changes from green to the cured state. When the leaf becomes yellow it is "killed" by drying, so it can change no more. Hence the high 170-degree temperature at the end, ensuring that no more chemical changes occur; the color is "set."

We would often gather as a family at the barn after supper and set around on the tobacco bench, lie in the hammocks made of sewn guano or fertilizer bags, and joke and carry on about the day, catch up on community gossip, and just in general enjoy the cool breeze and the company of the three giant oaks that had seen so many more just like us. The sweet smell of the tobacco curing, the night insects and tree frogs exploding in full song, the endless starry sky, all served to distract you from the often-harsh reality of everyday farm life. Families were tight, bonds were strong, and all was right with the world, since soon, very soon, the first money of the year, however meager, would begin to trickle in.

I was just a kid, five years old or so, when everyone left but me and Grandaddy. That was the magical time, just us "men" left to stay up all night and tend and stoke the fire: check the thermometer inside the barn from time to time and either add logs or take the long fire poker and spread out the embers to make the fire burn cooler. He taught me my ABCs and to count, or I was free to ask questions, any questions; it seemed he could answer them all. I was the chosen one, the one he used to help him work all night. It was my job to make sure he didn't fall asleep and I could do it well. We would lie in the hammock looking at the stars as the fire would crackle and pop and give its eerie red-glow color to the oaks and high grass. Grandma would cook extra biscuits and middlin'', and sometime around midnight we would go fix biscuits of Damson preserves, hand-churned butter, and middlin''. Most often we would grab a couple of "oatmeal glasses" and put ice water in a big quart Mason jar to take back with us.

The dew would fall, and the night air would get chilly. We rested in the hammocks or on the tobacco bench under blankets made of guano bags as well, which you had to vigorously shake to get the spiders to finally turn loose of. You didn't want to be too comfortable lest you fall asleep, and you couldn't do that because the heat had to be monitored constantly. The most critical time was when you needed to raise the heat in the barn toward the end of the curing process; if the tobacco still had green in it and you went up with the heat too quickly, the green was forever stuck, and the tobacco would never cure out golden. Or worst yet, you could end up with green stems inside beautiful golden leaves, which would kill the market value. Too much heat with the tobacco already dry, and the whole barn could catch on fire. They were tense nights sometimes.

I remember Grandaddy curing tobacco for neighbors whose barns had burned, and although, when they asked him what they owed him, he would always say, "You don't owe me a thing, I might need your help one day," at the end a smoke-cured shoulder, ham, or middlin'' would somehow appear in our smokehouse and no one would know how it had gotten there.

Now, fifty-three years later, I realize just how much of the character traits that I take for granted came from tobacco: perseverance, teamwork, discipline, responsibility, and toughness, both physical and especially mental. I have to thank tobacco because the best, and in some cases earliest, memories etched into the ever-winding fields of my aging mind still remain, and, like it or not, it was tobacco that put them there.

Grandaddy

My Grandaddy, William, and Grandma, Sarah, were married young. Never have I known two people who shared the same capacity for the long days required to scrape a living from the red clay of a share-cropped farm.

Pleasure for my Grandaddy was hunting and fishing. He and Dillard Baisey, our neighbor across the road, fished together whenever possible, in a small johnboat. Rheingold beer for refreshment, and homemade dough balls my Grandma or Mrs. Baisey had made and earthworms were bait for carp, catfish, bream, and bass. The Meherrin or Nottaway Rivers, Buggs Island Lake, and farm ponds were their playgrounds. Fish of any type were a real treat, because meat for us was one commodity that was hard to come by. I remember my Grandaddy mostly squirrel hunting. I know he did turkey hunt and hunt rabbit and bobwhite, but it was squirrel that I remember most.

My Grandaddy welcomed me into the world, taught me to count and what was right and wrong, and I followed him around like a little dog. He praised me when I did well in school because school was one area most of the family had little experience with. When he died in 1963 on Thanksgiving Day, I think I died with him. I know my respect for religion, my hopes and dreams and feelings hardened and never really softened again after that. I have known and loved one of the finest pastors, Harvey Duke, that this country has ever known, in my opinion. He baptized me at age thirty-three, and for a few months I felt the warmth of salvation and then … it died again like a coal in a woodstove. It will still occasionally flicker but I don't think will ever flame again … and yet … I still hope it will.

My First Car

Seems like every childhood memory for me, good or bad, has a tree involved, from roaming the woods behind Grandma's, to the elderberry bush at the packhouse, to the big oaks at the tobacco barns. This memory is no different. Uncle Page had a giant post oak in his front yard. It was like a magnet; everyone gathered under it in chairs on hot summer days. It was where you placed your head in your hands as you counted to a hundred for hide-and-seek, and it was a welcome playground when it was raining too hard to play in the yard.

We were headed to Uncle Page's for some of his special brand of Brunswick stew, a Southside Virginia staple. I was the first out of the car and I bounded for the big oak where Uncle Page stood over the stewpot. He had on his pith helmet — a big hard-shell "Smokey the Bear"-looking hat, only the top is rounded and not creased — and faded bib overalls. He had the helmet pushed back and was wiping his brow with an old red bandana handkerchief.

"What you doing, boy?" he said and tried to grab me but I wasn't falling for that one.

The smell in the air was nearly as thick as the stew itself! In the big cast-iron pot, pork, chicken, deer, rabbit, and squirrel bubbled, nestled among fresh garden vegetables, tomatoes, corn, and butter beans. The sweet smell of oak and hickory logs was carried on the light breeze from the wood fire, now white-hot below the big black stewpot. You couldn't escape the heat from the fire; it emanated from every angle and had coated the sides of the big vessel in thick white ash.

It was a long labor; he had most likely been there since just after midnight the night before. He used a big hand-carved hickory boat paddle to stir the stew to keep it from sticking on the bottom and ensure even cooking. Every few minutes he would stick the paddle in and pull it out at an angle. Usually a few bones would come out with it, captured on the side of the paddle, and he would toss them into the thick honeysuckle at the edge of the yard.

We had barely finished mingling when Aunt Juanita called, "Y'all come eat," and the line formed for the thick bowls of steaming-hot stew. Brunswick stew, if you have never had it, is a meal that needs to be experienced. Thick enough to eat with a fork, the stew was the consummated marriage of the meats and vegetables; one is almost indistinguishable from the other and the taste crosses the barriers of time, uniting the simplicity of generations past to the reality of generations present.

After a sumptuous meal of stew and light bread, as we called it — just sliced store-bought loaf bread was all it was — we would make homemade ice cream. He had an old big wooden ice cream churn made from white oak barrel staves. It must have been an heirloom from someone, somewhere; I was sure it had pleasured many people in its lifetime. The crank was stained a dark, slick rust color and it looked almost too old to turn. Aunt Juanita would fill it with fresh milk, cream, eggs, vanilla flavoring … in all honesty I don't remember the ingredients, I just know the end result! It was kid powered; we took turns winding the big crank handle that turned the stainless-steel cylinder around, which rock salt had been mixed with ice, to make it "super cold." It always seemed to be an eternity before it was ready! A sweet vanilla aroma hit you between the eyes the minute the lid was removed, and then the biting cold hit you between the eyes again in the form of an ice cream headache! Boy, was it good!

The men would usually ride up to Hines Store, for a cold beer, while we ate ice cream.

Uncle Page's daughters — Carolyn and Joyce — and I had been playing together most of the afternoon. I was about five years old, I think. Carolyn was a couple of years older than I was. She, like Joyce, was a pretty girl, thin with short black hair, and an old print dress. Joyce was only a year or so older than Carolyn, also thin, with auburn hair and a faded print dress as well. We were all barefoot. Like all boys and girls when very young, we faced the age-old dilemma: what do you play? We ended up playing the only games we boys and girls had in common: hide and seek, dodge ball, Simon says.

Aunt Juanita had found an old toy car. She said she didn't know where it had come from. It was down to the metal, the paint long ago worn off, but it still had four hard rubber tires and they turned! She said I could "have it to play with." Car in hand, I did just that, for hours. If only this story could stop right now, what a joy that would be!

When it came time to go, I simply stuck the old car in the pocket of my bib overalls. After all, she had said it was mine "to play with."

We left and went home. I went to well-worn patch of red clay back of Grandma's and started playing car.

Daddy walked by on the way to the outhouse and asked, "What you got there?" I showed him the car. "What are you doing with that?" he asked.

"Got it from Aunt Juanita," I answered.

"Stole it from Aunt Juanita, you mean," he said.

That I had stolen it had never crossed my mind. I told him what she said again, that I could "have it to play with."

He walked off and when he returned said, "Bring the car and come on with me." He stopped by the house and told Grandma I had "stolen the car from Juanita's" and we were going to take it back.

I had never known shame, and didn't know the name of it then, just the feeling. It was the kind of deep-down stomachache you get with the flu, and I knew it wouldn't go away anytime soon. I felt like a piece of old moldy bread, just something nobody wants. I couldn't look at Grandma's face as I walked by the screen door. I could only imagine what was going through her mind, and with a sighing reluctance I climbed into the old Ford.

The trip went far too quickly. As we drove into the yard Uncle Page and Aunt Juanita were relaxing in the old wicker-bottom chairs on the long, covered front porch.

Aunt Juanita stood up and immediately asked, "Is something wrong, is everyone OK?"

Daddy said, "Yeah. Go tell her what you did."

I walked over to the porch with my head hung like a whipped puppy and said, "I took your car home."

"Tell her what you really did," he said, matter-of-factly.

All the pent-up emotion just spewed out; it was more than I could hold in. I started sobbing uncontrollably and said through staggered breaths, "I stole your car, Aunt Juanita."

She looked as heartbroken as I felt. She came off the porch, walked over to the car and told Daddy, "William, it's OK, he can have it; it's just an old toy car. I don't even know where it came from."

"No," he said, "he has to learn his lesson."

I gave it back to her and walked back to the car just completely broken.

When we got home, he said, "Go cut a switch" and handed me his pocketknife.

"What for?" I asked.

"You know what for," he replied.

I got a little finger-sized sweet gum branch about two feet long, stripped the leaves and took it back. I had long ago learned that if the switch you brought back was too small, they would go pick a bigger one themselves.

He grabbed my arm and spun me around and started on my legs and hips. It hurt, and it burned, but I couldn't cry. I had already been hurt far worse than this would ever hurt.

"This don't seem to bother you much," he said. "Don't you know what you did? You don't even care enough to cry."

I hadn't realized at the time that I had done wrong, but now I knew I had. I had apologized for it, and from humiliation and shame I had truly learned my lesson. I didn't cry, and I would never cry again at another spanking, and they stopped.

I would never second-guess Daddy, or the spanking. All I know is that no lesson has ever stuck with me more. I explained to Grandma why I had done it and that I knew it was a mistake, and she asked if I knew it was still wrong, mistake or not, and I told her I did. It was a harsh lesson at an early age, and yet it was the cornerstone of a foundation that would teach me right from wrong forever. Many times in life when tempted to do things I knew were wrong, I would think of that little car. And still today.

I apologized to Aunt Juanita almost every visit after that, until she finally just told me, "Jimmy, you quit that, that's over and gone."

But it was not over and gone … It will never be over and gone.

Trees

Down in the mule pasture was a black gum tree. I liked to climb it because it was tall, probably thirty-five feet, and the limbs grew at irregular intervals, making it easy to scale. Grandaddy liked it for another reason though. The limbs and twigs of a black gum are very fibrous and do not break easily. He would get a pencil-sized twig about seven inches long and twist and twist until it popped off. The roughed end he would then dip into salt or baking soda and use for a toothbrush. People who dipped snuff would keep one handy too, since the end would also pick up just the right amount of snuff to place between cheek and gum. Old-time beekeepers used hollow sections of black gum trees as a natural "hive tree" partly because the flowers of the black gum are sweet and make an especially good honey. A pretty tree as well, the black gum is the first to turn color in fall and the leaves burn a bright red. They are somewhat transparent and when the morning sun hits one, it almost looks like it glows.

Grandaddy and Mr. Baisey would make locust beer at times. I don't know the exact recipe, but it was a simple process. You just took the black, ripened locust pods and broke them up in a keg or crock, one layer a few inches deep; then you added a layer of cut, ripe persimmons, and two cups of blackstrap molasses; and then you poured enough boiling water on them to cover everything and let it sit for three or four days. Strain it through a sheet and chill. I thought it tasted nasty, kind of like drinking tobacco juice.

The thorns on locust trees when they are old and gray can be broken off and used as nails, and the Indians preferred this wood for bow making because of its strength and elasticity.

A lot of sassafras trees were in the wood line; sometimes we would make root beer by tearing or crushing the leaves and pouring boiling water over them just enough to cover. Let it sit off the heat about twenty minutes or so, then just strain out the leaves, chill the liquid, and, if you had it, add a little honey and sparkling water for fizz. Or you could pull up small sassafras trees and use the roots; they make even better root beer. Wash the roots and then boil in just enough water to cover, for about twenty minutes. You could use the roots over again. And you could chew on sassafras twigs and it would make your breath smell better.

We used the elderberry bush that grew by the packhouse to make "pop guns" and "water pistols." And Grandaddy and Mr. Baisey talked about drinking elderberry wine made from the small quarter-inch-or-so berries. I never saw them make any, but I do remember they said you had to cook the berries first and that the wine was particularly sweet. Quite a few folks made tomato wine, but we never did; it was cheaper just to buy it from someone's car trunk from the many peddlers who visited from time to time.

We had a persimmon tree and Grandaddy would eat the persimmons after they got frosted on and fell off the tree, if the wildlife didn't get them first. He said they were soft like jelly inside and tasted a lot like honey. I know Grandma said you could make jelly and jam with them but I don't think she liked it and never made any. I never tasted one because Grandaddy said if it wasn't ripe it would "turn your mouth inside out" and I didn't like the visual image I got from that one. I did use them in the rabbit box, but apple worked best of anything for that.

Dogwoods we always used for "grit shooters"; sling shots is what most folks call them. Seemed the dogwood just had more symmetrically shaped one-inch Y-shaped branch formations than most trees and were strong. If you could find an old red rubber inner tube from a truck blowout on the highway, you had a prize! The red rubber has some super strength and elasticity, and it would send a steel ball bearing through a thin piece of plywood.

We fed the acorns from the two big white oaks at the barns to the hogs to fatten them up. Neither the hogs or the deer would eat the red oak acorns; they were just too bitter.

The little cap that held the acorn made a good whistle. You put it between your thumbs, the open end facing you, then you covered up about a third of the opening with each thumb forming a Y shape, with the open third of the Y in the center. Pucker your lips and blow hard like you were trying to blow out candles on a cake three feet away. The knuckles on your thumbs should rest on your lips. You will have a little trial and error, but when you blow it right, you will know it.

Grass made a fun whistle too. Get a piece of grass a quarter inch wide at least. Pick the grass as close to the ground as possible. Place it between your thumbs with the grass flat against the back of your thumbs, thumbs facing you. You will notice a space between your thumbs underneath the knuckles and above where your thumb joins your hands. Place that space to your lips and blow. You should hear a shrieking, piercing whistle.

We used hickory wood to smoke our meats. Although we had hickory trees on the farm, the easiest thing to do was go to the axe handle factory in Kenbridge. They discarded as many handles as they used, due to flaws, grain going the wrong way, holes in the wood, warping. You could get a truckload for four dollars and we usually got eight or ten handles that were good enough to use and burned the rest in the woodstove or used them to smoke meats.

Indians used to crush hickory nuts and boil them in water. A cream-colored oil rose to the top, was skimmed off, and was stored as a paste that was used on corn cakes or hoecakes like we use butter.

Indians also used the white oak acorns I mentioned before. They were dried, shelled, rinsed, and then ground into a meal that was used as flour and as a thickener for soups and stews. Acorns can keep up to two years if kept dry.

Wild grapes called muscadines, or scuppernong by some, were plentiful and used in jelly, preserves, and wine. Muscadine wine is usually pretty sweet because sugar is added during fermenting and the grape itself has natural sugars.

Likewise, blackberries and dewberries were usually plentiful. Dewberries grow on the ground instead of on upright thorny stems like blackberries and are sweeter and softer; it's hard to pack many together without squashing them. Grandma mostly made a baked dumpling with them, but she would make preserves on occasion.

By far her favorite thing was damsons, which she used to make preserves, jellies, and jams. PBJ for me always meant damson jelly. I had to develop a taste for grape jelly years later; it just didn't taste right.

Hoecakes

Hoecakes have a long history. Long before the arrival of Europeans, Native Americans were making them, from ground Indian corn, and cooking them on hot stones over a fire. Called *jonican* by some natives, the corn cakes became known as "journey cakes," partly because they were easily made, easily transported, and held up well. From that name, "johnny cakes" sprang. Other names are corn pone, referring to the ground corn they are made from, and ashcakes, because when cooked over an open campfire with flying ashes, the ashes often became an ingredient. In the South, however, they were often made right in the fields. The hoes used by fieldhands had a wide face and the corn cakes were cooked right on the face of a hoe held over an open flame. Therefore, the name "hoecake." If the hoe had been gradually warmed, the hoecakes would not stick to the surface.
Grandma used a tiny pinch of sugar in hers.

1 cup of fine, stone-ground yellow cornmeal
1/2 cup flour
1/2 teaspoon salt
Pinch of sugar
Cold water
Bacon grease or lard

-Combine the dry ingredients and mix well. The flour is optional but it improves the texture of the cake.
-Add just enough cold water to make a stiff but fluid batter.
-Gradually warm the cast-iron frying pan; this way the hoecakes are less likely to stick.
-Add enough bacon grease or lard to coat the bottom well.
-Drop tablespoons of batter, usually two to three per cake and cook slowly until brown on each side, 3 to 5 minutes depending on the heat of the woodstove.

Grandaddy Gholson

Doctor's visits were rare, for anything.

I remember a late fall afternoon at Grandaddy Gholson's, my mother's father. He was a thinly muscled, wiry man, with a wrinkled, knowing face, framed by wire-rimmed glasses. He walked with a slight slouch, likely from a bad back. He had gray, receding hair and often wore suspenders and matching gray work shirt and pants. And he was intensely religious. He talked like I would imagine the pioneers of old talking. A customer walking into his store would be greeted with, "Good afternoon, brother. How may I be of humble service to you?"

He had married again after my grandmother's death. His new wife, Annie, was also thin, gray hair wound into a tight bun at the back. She looked as if she had been pretty when younger but now she just looked subdued, like life had taken from her all it could except her very breath. She wore mainly dark print dresses and always a sweater, even in summer. She canned incessantly, everything they grew and anything they could barter for from a neighbor's garden as well. She even canned pork. I had never seen it done and it looked despicable in the big Mason jars, large, cooked chunks of off-white, nondescript meat. Whenever we ate there, although it was never voiced, I always got the feeling we were an inconvenience they could not afford. Annie was, however, an excellent cook and on the occasion when we stayed for a meal, the food was on par with anyone's.

I was always amazed by the grace Grandaddy Gholson would say at each meal: "Our Heavenly Father, we humbly thank you for the bounty you have provided this table, the fellowship of our gathered family and friends, the joy and blessing of a healthy body and mind. Our Father, we ask that you use our minds and bodies to glorify your spirit, to spread the truth of your word, and to shine the promised light of salvation, paid for by the blood of your only son. It is in his name, Jesus Christ, that we ask this blessing, in the name of the Father, the Son, and the Holy Ghost."

He would then say "Amen" and if you did not respond in

kind, he would pause, and say, "Jimmy, I don't believe I heard you say "Amen,' " and he would wait until you did. Man, woman, or child.

He was still operating a small, unpainted, wood-framed, two-story, five-room store at Barnes Junction, Virginia. Two old gas pumps were out front, with the big "bubble" top, "Flying A" faded into near oblivion on the glass. The drive was covered with bottle caps and gravel, and two ever-present mud holes. As you entered, there was a tall pot-bellied woodstove in the center of one giant room that ran the entire length of the building. Just behind the stove a large wooden counter ran the entire length of the room as well. The counter had a "lift up" so you could go between the large front room and the two back rooms. On the counter were an old hand-crank cash register and a few jars of penny cookies — shortbread, ginger snaps, oatmeal; some baskets of penny candy — Mary Janes, bubble gum, chocolate "coins" in the gold wrapper, caramels, peanut butter logs; several small racks of Gordon's Potato Chips; boxes of candy bars — Milky Way, Clark Bar, Hershey's, Baby Ruth, Zagnut, bubble gum cigars, with just two or three in each box. The front room of the store on each side was cavernous and bare. A couple of shelves on a back wall contained maybe ten kinds of canned meats and vegetables — Bunker Hill Beef Stew, Old Prairie Oil Sausage, Banner Breakfast Sausage, Sauer's Pork Brains, Luck's pinto beans and navy beans, turnip greens, lima beans, and some yeast in muted, faded labels. The floor was bare wooden plank, so old the edges were rounded and it moved up and down as you walked on it. I would guess the whole place contained less than two hundred dollars' worth of inventory.

Their bedroom was to the right at the back of the store, behind the counter, and the dining room and kitchen combined were the room to the left. Just behind the dining room table and against the wall was a stairway that led to two dark, dank bedrooms upstairs. A double bed and bedpan in each room and nothing more, no dresser drawers, no pictures, nothing. A bedspread nailed to the wall served as a door between the two rooms. An old quilt and faded blanket on each bed and only one pillow per bed. A plate glass window of about two feet by eighteen inches at each end gave the only outside light.

There was an old outhouse way back down a small, weed-choked footpath back of the store. Daddy had gone to buy a beer down the road; Grandaddy Gholson would not sell alcohol and didn't like you to drink it and come around him. I was walking back of the outhouse in some thick honeysuckle, searching an old junkyard for old soda bottles I'd never heard of. Suddenly a searing, white-hot pain shot across the big toe on my left foot. I had stepped on a broken Mason jar; the fresh red blood was still glistening off its jagged edge. My foot was sliced from the bottom of my sole on the outside, all the way across the toe and down to the sole inside my foot between the toes on the other. I remember the blood just gushing; it wouldn't stop.

I ran back to the house. There was no phone and no one there with an automobile. Grandaddy Gholson sat me in a chair and laid a rag under my foot to catch the blood. He told Annie to give me a sucker. A big cherry Tootsie Roll Pop was what she came back with.

He had her hold my toe tightly pressed together while he scooped black soot from the fireplace. Then with his thumb he packed the soot deep into the wound. Never have I felt such pain. But the bleeding stopped, and an old rag bandage was applied. When Daddy got back it was decided since it wasn't bleeding we would just leave it be. It swelled quite large, but never got infected.

I hobbled about for most of the rest of the summer to keep from busting the cut loose again. Today, more than fifty years later, the black band of soot, although faded into a more subtle blue, is still visible, with no permanent damage to the toe. A toe, by the way, that Mary Ann, my wife, says could still be used to "stomp out most forest fires."

Bobwhite

When you live hand-to-mouth there is a fine line between entertainment and necessity. The "mouth call" I guess would somehow fall into this category. We did not buy commercial game calls. We either made them, or just used our mouth and vocalized the call ourselves.

At dusk Grandaddy would sit on the porch and call "whippoorwill" and "bobwhite." He was so good I have seen bobwhite come out into the open and approach the porch where we sat. I have seen a bobwhite stand there, then walk back and forth completely puzzled as to where the heck the female bobwhite that Grandaddy was imitating had gone. The bobwhite would go back into the thick cover, only to have Grandaddy call him right back out, to stand there looking up, down, and sideways before walking off in a huff.

In the spring we would call crows and shoot them to keep them from eating freshly planted crops, and likely for sport as well, if the truth be known. Aside from the well-known three-note "caw, caw, caw," which is the alarm call for a crow, there were two others much more useful. Crows have a bad temperament and love to fight, especially on drizzly dreary days. We would play on this trait and use the "fight call" to bring them in and then the "wounded crow" call to keep them there. The fight call, hard to describe in words, consists of four notes, two long ones — "caaaaaaaw, caaaaaaaw" — followed by two quick, back-to-back "caw, caw." It carried an unmistakable message to a crow: *Hey, want some of this? I don't think so, chicken boy!* Once the crows came in to the call and you had shot a couple, they were ready to leave; crows are very intelligent. But then you would switch to the wounded crow call, a painful, low-toned "owwwwww, owwwwww, ahhhhhhh, ahhhh." Crows won't abandon a wounded comrade; they come back and peck him to death, but they don't leave him. A wounded crow attracts predators, which endangers the whole flock; it's a built-in survival instinct.

Turkeys were called by mouth or with a wing call. These

were made by taking the long, hollow wing bone of a turkey, removing the firing cap from a spent shotgun shell, inserting the bone through the resulting hole, and sealing the hole with pitch or tar. The wing call was then placed under the tongue and sucked to create the "yelp" of a hen turkey.

Turkeys have a complex language; they do more than gobble: they cluck, cry, purr, and cackle, and each sound, along with the number of times it is made, has a meaning. The male gobble is purely a mating call, but a hen turkey yelps, and the number of yelps determines her message. Four to five yelps indicate a hen turkey feeding. Thirty or more strung together in a row indicate a lost turkey or a hen turkey looking for "companionship." Combine making this call with scratching the leaves near you gently with your hand and a love-struck gobbler was sure to swoon over your way in full strut, tail feathers flared like an Indian headdress. It is an adrenaline rush and many a hunter has gotten excited and shot the turkey with an empty gun, just simply forgetting to chamber a shell. The key to getting a turkey was to be perfectly still. Someone who is a bad caller but good at remaining still will kill more birds than a good caller who shows movement.

No one seems to know why, but a male turkey will answer thunder; if you are hunting and it thunders, you will know right away if a male is anywhere near. Come to think of it, I guess turkeys had eHarmony-dot-com long before we thought of it!

Strawberries

I lay sprawled on my back in the cool greenness of ankle-high clover, half covered in ants and yet still enjoying the summer shade graciously offered by the wide limbs of the umbrella tree in Grandma's front yard. Barefooted, tattered blue jeans painted by the red clay dirt, and no shirt. I laughed to myself as I surveyed the nastiness of my situation. I was, as Aunt Sis would say, a "true mess."

Crawfish are to bass are like peanuts and popcorn are to humans: they just can't get enough, so to please the fish at Gayle's Pond, I had walked the branch, hunting crawfish all the way from the spring behind Old Man Conner's house down to our old tobacco plant bed. The crawfish on this day had reigned supreme, and all I had gained were the mosquito whelps that spotted my chest and face. Inspired by an early-morning *Popeye* cartoon, I was now covered in elaborate tattoos of an anchor, barbed wire, circles, crosses, and dots all over my arms, legs, stomach, and forehead. All stained by pokeberry juice and fashioned by my bright-red fingertips and nails. I had the unsettling feeling that come nightfall I would pay for these treasures with a switch or the belt, but night was a long ways off and maybe it would all wear a little clean by then, I reasoned. My left hand was still swollen from an early-morning red wasp that was successful in attacking and stinging its aggressor, after I had unmercifully used a tobacco stick to knock down its nest, hanging just under the eaves of the smokehouse. My right thumb still contained last week's splinter from a chunk of stove wood and was now infected, and I knew I would have to undergo the needle, made red-hot by a match before being used to remove the wooden sliver and free the flesh from the infection.

Ever been digging fishing worms and find a grub worm, white, thumb-sized, and curled with a brown head? Well, what they turn into was then in a flying frenzy over my head. Almost three feet off the ground, buzzing as hard and fast as he could flap his wings, was a metallic green June bug, tethered with a sewing thread tied to his leg. I had intended to let him go if his leg didn't break off and free him first, but he grew tired and landed, and before I could jerk the thread to revive his flight, a chicken's peck ended his confinement. A white "mayonnaise" covered the outside of the chicken's beak, the unmistakable signature of a June bug's interior.

The "Watkins Man" and his small car were parked in the driveway and I knew Grandma was buying a bottle of "vitims" and listening to road gossip. The "Watkins Man" knew everything about everyone and although Grandma wasn't one to gossip, she did like to know how all the neighbors were doing, who was sick or hurt, whose sons had been drafted, and how other folks' crops were doing.

"See you, see yer" and "see you, see yer" broke the silence as two male meadowlarks began a vocal duel. A meadowlark fights first with song and if there is no decisive winner of the "song battle," they will lock feet and peck each other until there is a victor. I could tell from the single song I now heard that this fight had ended peacefully.

School was over. I had two months off. I was too small to work in the tobacco much yet, so I was pretty much left to fend for myself, but still I had to pay for my transgressions. Somehow, it seemed like today my transgressions were many. Aside from the pokeberry mess, I had destroyed two bales of hay by doing belly flops off the framework of the mule trough into the hay pile, I had broken a rail on the tobacco slide, and I had torn the guano bag cloth that covered its sides when imitating a Chief "Wahoo" McDaniel's wrestling kick, and although both the wood and the bag had been rotten anyway, I knew payback for this would hurt. I was safe on the watermelon, I thought; I had taken it into the woods, busted it on a stump, and eaten till I had a stomachache, but I had covered it in leaves so no one would find it. Then it dawned on me the vine was still there with nothing on it; surely someone would know.

As I walked over toward the front porch and studied this dilemma in depth, I felt a piercing pain in the arch just in front of my left heel. When I looked down I saw a big black spider slither under the leaves at the edge of the house. Oh God, I've been bitten by a black widow. The bite hurt worse with every step, and I knew I would soon be dead. Instinctively I sat down and grabbed my foot for a look. Imbedded in the flesh was a huge, dried thorn. As I removed the thorn, dark red blood flowed freely. Blood was still a scary thing but between a spider bite and blood this was the best by far. Knowing it was just a thorn was sweet relief indeed!

Uncle Bo came out from his afternoon nap, arms stretched and yawning almost as wide as Old Bob, his bird dog, could. He put on his tan work hat and headed for his '32 Ford truck.

"Want to go to the store?" he asked.

I never turned down a chance to go to Hines Store.

"Can I ride in the back?" I asked.

"Long as you sit on the floor and not the fender wall," he replied. "I ain't having you fall off my truck. Ought not to take you anywhere that nasty," he added, as he closed his door, then slammed it two more times before the latch finally caught.

There's just something special about riding in the back of a pickup truck down a dirt road, the roadside trees little more than a blur, the gravel crunching underneath, wind blowing through your hair, big dirt cloud churning behind you like the water wake of a boat, even at a slow speed. The only problem comes when the truck stops and the choking dust cloud catches up. Even with no one else in sight anywhere Uncle Bo always obeyed the law and came to a complete stop, a stop that now seemed in slow motion as the stifling cloud settled in on me, clothes, hair, face all consumed in a sea of red. I sneezed, coughed, gagged, and thankfully again we were moving. As I shook my head I could feel the grit and sand roll off my hair and down onto my neck and bare arms. We stopped at Hines Store under the big pin oak tree out front. The shade and breeze were welcoming.

"Go on, git you a popsicle," he said. "I know you want one."

As we walked in the store and my eyes adjusted to the darkness, I was temporarily blinded, and off to my left someone said, "Boy, my mamma would have tanned my hide if I was as covered in pokeberry juice as you are."

My adjusting vision revealed a big man with a wide smile and a big belly, in bib overalls and a white T-shirt, a red bandana handkerchief tied around his neck, and a large straw hat on his head. The hat had a dark piece of green plastic all along the front of the rim and when bent down acted as sunglasses do in shielding your eyes in the fields. Crowder's Store, where Daddy worked, sold them. It was Billy Wright, one of Uncle Bo's friends.

Uncle Bo slid the top of the metal drink box back and pulled out an ice-crusted short-bottle Coke, popped the top on the opener on the side of the drink box, and stopped to talk to someone pouring Lance peanuts into his Pepsi on top of the old pot-bellied wood heater. I waffled back and forth between banana and chocolate but finally grabbed a Chocolate Fudgesicle and went outside to eat it sitting on the picnic table at the top of the hill by the side of the store. As I glanced behind me toward the surface road, the dirt road we lived on, something suddenly spread its arms and legs and soared effortlessly from a vine to its nest. It was a flying squirrel. Paul Whitlock and I were the only ones who knew they were back there, as far as I knew, and we had told no one because we didn't want to see them killed. I had never seen any others anywhere, even at Dixie's Bridge and the hardwood bottomland of the river.

Uncle Bo suddenly emerged from the front door and I instinctively started down the hill toward him.

"Let's ride to the Powell Place," Uncle Bo said.

I liked going there. The Powell Place was part of our farm, "our farm" meaning Mrs. Johnson's land. There was considerable acreage on it and we raised mostly corn there, big winding fields on both sides of the road. I had always liked telling folks the Powell Place was "ours"; most everyone knew where it was.

On the right side of the road as it meandered downward toward the creek was the actual "Powell Place," a one-room building made of weathered, rough-hewn wood that had never seen paint or stain. Inside there were small-slatted walls, the hardwood grayed slats only about an inch wide, plaster oozing between every crack, as if the building had never been completed. I had seen work like that in only one or two other old houses, all in disrepair. A rusted wood heater with no flue leaned lazily to one side on the partially rotted floorboards of the front room. Two small pane glass windows, sans glass, provided enough light to show an old porcelain slop jar lying in the corner and a few old blue Mason canning jars lying on one side. I thought it sad that this was all that remained of some family's life here. The house was now overgrown with honeysuckle, poison oak, and sumac vines.

On most of my visits a large black snake lounged on the cedar handrails of the rusted tin-covered back porch. Reluctantly, almost disgustedly, he would slowly slither until he dropped off and sashayed underneath the vine-choked floor.

Out back was an exposed well with no frame that always drew me like a magnet, even though I had been whipped several times for leaning over it to look down. These old wells were dug by hand and lined with fieldstone all the way to the surface of the water and they fascinated me.

The creek was in the valley between the two hills, just a hundred or so yards below. It was a good hole to fish for hornehead, beam, and catfish, and deep enough to swim in... but you couldn't swim anymore, Daddy had said, because "sorry bastards" had thrown broken glass in the water.

There were nearby springs in the bottoms, and arrowheads were often found in the cornfields here, so the place had been a comfort to people long before us and the Powells. I had always asked, and no one knew, who exactly "the Powells" were. The building was dilapidated and looking ready to fall even in my earliest memories, so it had to be a very old homestead.

The dirt road was rough. It hadn't been scraped by the state in a while and my butt jarred quite painfully up and down from time to time. We rode to the top of the next hill, where Herbert Hines, who owned the store, lived in a big white framed one-story house, turned left, and headed downhill to cross the creek yet again, toward Forksville and the big white two-room school that was part of Uncle Page's farm, on Mr. Rogers's land. We pulled in and came to a squeaking stop, parking just under the huge white oak trees to the right of the school building.

The school was big, only one room but almost two stories high, with a huge A-framed tin roof amd windows that seemed to cover the whole side from just above floor level to the ceiling on both sides. I had never seen so much glass in a building. It had two oversized entrance doors side by side. Daddy had said it was first through sixth grades taught. Each few rows of church pews held a different class and the same teacher taught all six classes. It had a couple of outhouses out back: a girls' and boys'.

Uncle Bo said, "Come on and let's take a walk and a look."

We lazily strode down the weed-filled trail between the big oaks toward the tobacco fields, and suddenly a covey of bobwhite exploded into flight and startled us both. Bobwhite usually fly just off the ground and only a short ways unless they feel a real threat and these did just that, sailing just barely out of sight and into the woods' edge. We could see them scuttling toward the leaves and cover as we rounded the bend.

"Me and Old Bob will see you again come hunting season," Uncle Bo said to no one in particular.

He veered off and headed toward a thick patch of green weeds and bent down on his knee. As I glanced over at him, I saw the sunlight sheen from a bright red glint in his cupped hand. Strawberries!

"There's a wild strawberry patch here," he said.

We sat in the warm glow of the mid-afternoon sun and ate ripe strawberries, as sweet as the day is long, until we both had our fill. He took off his hat and loaded it to the rim with red, ripe berries to take back home to Grandma.

"Might make some strawberry cream," he said.

Homemade strawberry ice cream. Now that would be a treat for sure, I thought.

"When you git home, put some dirt on them pokeberry stains with just a little bit of water and rub hard and they will come out," he said. "Then rinse off good with water and take a bath in the wash-pan."

"How you know that?" I asked.

"Don't matter how I know it," he said.

I climbed in the cab of the truck with him, and we drove toward the slowly sinking sun and headed home. Uncle Bo didn't say another word.

Wagon Trains And Mules

It was late January. The temperatures had been in the teens for days. Both houses — Grandma's and Daddy's — just stayed uncomfortably cold, with one exception: when you stood just inches away, with your butt facing the wood heater. Wood heaters can fill a room with warm, radiant heat, but the fire has to be tended constantly, ashes raked out into an "ash pan," usually just an old dented wash-pan on the floor, and the coals must be stoked from time to time with the "fire poker." A fire poker was just a long, black metal J-shaped rod that resembled a long skinny fishhook, with a rounded handle. Leave it in the red-hot coals too long and you will find that, yes, it does conduct a lot of heat; you could get branded!

It was just after eight o'clock, so I had gone over to Daddy's house to sleep. Night was the only time I spent with Momma and Daddy. Every minute of every day, I was following Grandaddy like a shadow, playing checkers with Grandma, or traipsing around in the woods that surrounded the farm. I was still small enough that I could fit in the bed with Momma and Daddy so most of the night I was warm. We would fill the heater and get a roaring fire going, crackling and sparks flying out every opening. Sparks that you would nervously watch until they burned themselves out on the square tin mat under the wood heater. As the room started to chill you would just be drifting off in blissful slumber. You would instinctively pull the cover over your head and allow your breath to "heat" up the bed.

By morning, regardless of what you did, the little two-room, uninsulated house would be reminiscent of upper Siberia! You would wake up and see your breath fog just as it does outside. The pane glass windows would have crystalline ice so thick you could not see outside until the mid-morning sun burned it off. "Someone" needed to get up and start the fire, which was by now completely burned out. If you were "living right," there might be a stray ember or two hanging on to a faint glimmer of life, just enough to make the "lightwood" blaze and start the day's warmth anew. The trouble was, who would do it? Not me; I wasn't allowed to play with fire. Momma would say, "I just don't know how to do it right," and Daddy would say, "Ain't no use getting up yet; we got thirty more minutes."

I usually slept in my clothes, but even then you have to get up and put your shoes and socks on. It had to be in the teens at best in the house. It was kind of like swimming at the river; the water was going to be ice cold from the constant shade so the only thing to do was just run, jump in, and get it over with. So that's what I did: jumped up, grabbed my shoes and socks, haphazardly pulled them on, tied a mangled knot, snatched up my jacket and hat, and by then my teeth were chattering.

"Put a few pieces of firewood in the heater," Daddy said.

I grudgingly obliged. I swung the hinged lid open and dropped in two small pieces of kindling and a piece of stove wood. Gray dust swirled up and out along, with a few small sparks.

"I guess we must be livin' right," I mused.

I grabbed the ice-cold doorknob, opened the thin wooden front door, and stepped out into a meat locker; geez, it was bone chilling. I ran like a bullet to Grandma's. Rattler came out from under the house and stretched, back arched downward and legs touching the frosted ground. I managed a quick "pat on the head," still on the fly, as I sped past him.

The screen door was still latched from the night before. I knocked and yelled. Nothing; she was in the kitchen and couldn't hear. I ran to the back door and when I grabbed the handle it opened. Whew! Inside I took my hat off and it was toasty warm!

"Mawning," she said.

"Mawning, Grandma," I replied.

"Wash them nasty hands," she commanded. She was standing in her faded, brown-checked handmade dress with just a button-up sweater on, one button in the center connected.

She picked up a stick of stove wood off the woodbox to add to the fire. The woodbox to the right of the stove was brimming with stove wood and "kindling," long thin pieces of "lightwood" split from old heartwood pine stumps. You could just touch a match to it and it would blaze in a white-hot fire. Grandma would put a little crumbled-up paper in the bottom, a few pieces of lightwood crisscrossed on top of it, and then a few thin sticks of firewood, and with a single match she would have a fire going in seconds. After it "caught" she would add stove wood as needed.

The old aluminum coffee percolator, sporting numerous scrapes and dents, was announcing "booboobbloop," "cwshtt," "booboobbloop," "cwshtt," and the aroma of good old Eight O'Clock Coffee filled the kitchen. Grandma kept close watch on it, since "Coffee boiled is coffee spoiled."

I was early. She had finished kneading the dough in the big wooden bread pan. A cup of flour makes five "fat" biscuits, and she usually added two teaspoons of baking powder, a pinch of salt, and two tablespoons of lard. As soon as the flour becomes wet it forms gluten, and the more you knead it, the tougher the biscuit is. She had rolled it out and was cutting out biscuits with the rim of an "oatmeal glass." The square Formica-topped table was already set with dishes, silverware, and cups. There was a big saucer of fried fatback already cooked and I munched on a salty, crunchy slice while I waited on the biscuits. The butter patty with Grandma's signature "star" mashed into the top with the edge of a big wooden spoon was on the table softening.

Grandaddy hustled in, shivering. "Only two more left," he said.

He held aloft a long white bag about the length and thickness of a man's forearm, tied at the top with tobacco twine. The outside of the bag looked like dried blood and the bag itself had shriveled and wrinkled to fit the form of the fresh sausage inside. We stuffed fresh ground sausage in these bags, which Grandma had sown from old white cloth, and hung them in the smokehouse to cure, not from smoke but just through natural dehydration in the cold.

Grandma opened the top, reached down a few inches, and squeezed out a chunk. She repeated the process all the way to the end of the bag. The bag went in the fire, where it sizzled and popped. We rarely had any garbage; cans were really all. Bottles went back to the store, jars were used to put preserves and jelly in, and the rest was burned in an old, rusted, 55-gallon drum, or if edible went as table scraps to the hogs.

The sausage had a lingering pinkness to it, and the smell, even with the sausage uncooked, was one of thick sage and pepper. The yellow seeds of the cayenne pepper pods used as seasoning were prominent. They both, Grandaddy and Grandma, liked it hot, and I mean not a hot for the timid: it was hot! Coffee when

swallowed after sausage seemed to accentuate the heat.

The wispy blue smoke rose from the sizzling sausage patties as Grandma cooked the eggs. Sunny-side up, two on my plate and Grandma's, three or four on Grandaddy's and Uncle Bo's. I lathered a biscuit with the juice from the pear preserves; everyone else liked the preserves themselves, but the juice to me tasted like honey. A thick smear of soft butter from the now softened patty, and I was ready.

Uncle Bo and Grandma "saucered" their coffee. Both could somehow hold the cup and saucer together, gently pouring coffee from cup to saucer and "ssslllllllurrrp." It was a noisy way to drink. I just blew on mine to cool it. Another bad or good thing about percolated coffee, depending on your perspective, was that it was usually scalding.

"We need to bust the rest of that firewood," Grandaddy said.

Uncle Bo just kept chewing on a sausage biscuit and contentedly nodded his head in agreement.

"Ward Bond died yesterday," Grandma said.

Grandaddy looked visibly shaken. "What happened?" he asked.

"Massive heart attack," Grandma replied.

Grandaddy got up and pushed his unfinished breakfast toward the center of the table; he looked almost ready to tear up.

"Who was Ward Bond?" I asked. "Where does he live?"

"He's the wagon master on *Wagon Train*," Grandma said, and then I remembered: it was Grandaddy's favorite TV show. In fact it was about the only thing he would watch.

"How old was he?" Grandaddy asked.

"Fifty-seven," said Grandma.

"That's a real shame, a real shame," he said. He just went outside and stood, one foot propped up on a big unsplit log and stared at the sunrise just beginning to set the eastern sky on fire.

"He won't ever watch it again," she said. "I know him. He just won't be able to do it."

Rattler stood on the porch gentling pushing on the screen door with his right front paw every few minutes; he was hungry too.

"Give him Grandaddy's breakfast," Grandma said. Rattler wolfed it down in two big bites and licked his lips. Then he ran for the chicken water in the tub by the well and slurped liked a mad man: the cayenne pepper in the sausage had gotten him; I knew what it was!

Uncle Page pulled in the yard on his old green GMC pickup, the kind with the short truck bed and running boards. He walked in the front door, not knowing Grandaddy was out back.

"H'air y'all doing?" he asked and instinctively grabbed a coffee cup.

"Want some breakfast?" Grandma asked.

"Just coffee. Me and Juanita done eat. Where's Daddy?"

"Out at the woodpile," she said.

"Old Ward Bond died," Uncle Page said.

"We's just talkin' 'bout that," Grandma replied.

"Grab him, Bo; let's git 'im," Uncle Page chuckled.

And Uncle Bo grinned and reached for me but I was up and out of the chair.

"Mule any better?" Uncle Page asked.

"Naw," said Uncle Bo, "still won't eat."

Tom, our mule, had lost weight and along with it the will to work. He had some age on him but not enough to be having these problems.

"I got some sorghum molasses. We can mix a little on his hay, maybe get him to eat," Uncle Page said.

When we got to the mule shed Old Tom was looking very feeble, cold and shivering, unsteady on his feet.

"He ain't going to make it," Uncle Page said; "we're probably going to have to put him out of his misery."

"Don't say nothing to Daddy yet," Uncle Bo said.

Losing the mule would be a big setback. Barner Jones's Livery Stable in La Crosse still sold them, but few folks now used them, and they were slim pickin's, just not of the best quality anymore. Even worse, we couldn't afford to buy one; the farm wasn't making much money as it was, and Mrs. Johnston just might not want to buy one either. This could be a very serious problem indeed.

Grandaddy still stood looking at the sunrise. TV was new, new to us anyway, yet the folks on it was just like family. Grandaddy was sure as sad as if he'd just lost family.

No one knew it for sure, though I guess we all suspected it, but in just a few days we would lose an animal that was part of the family too.

Tom

If anything, the weather seemed to be getting colder; there had been little if any let up. A lot of time was spent locating and busting firewood and lightwood for kindling. Finding lightwood was fun, kinda like a treasure hunt. I would walk the forest looking for old, weathered, rotted stumps or sections of stumps sticking up, sometimes just inches off the leaf litter. I had the ax with me, and when I found a stump I would kick it with my foot to see if it could be broken off, or chop it with the ax to see if it was "lightwood." Lightwood only came from pine stumps — the center, where the resin from the pine had collected, and it had a strong odor similar to Pine Sol. I carried an old burlap fertilizer bag to take home what I gathered. Usually I ended up just dragging it behind me, too full to carry. When you cook and heat with wood, you go through quite a bit of wood!

The two hogs had been killed weeks ago, and yet the bloodstains behind the now-mangled entrance to the pen still looked no more than a day or so old. Uncle Page told me how to do it, but I had no interest in trying any time soon. He said you imagined a line running from the right eye of the pig to its left ear and another line from the left eye to the right ear, where the two imaginary lines met in an "X" was where you shot. It was best to use a .22 shot. This would go through the brain, if done right the hog would drop immediately.

The day they had been killed he had rubbed the shoulders, hams, bellies, and loins with salt and then placed them in the salt box, starting with a salt layer on the bottom and then with a thin salt layer between each layer of meat all the way to the top. The hams, shoulders, and bellies, or middlin' as we called it, were now ready to be smoked in the new smokehouse he had recently built for us. They were removed from the salt and washed thoroughly in lukewarm water, patted dry, and rubbed with Morton's Sugar Cure and with black pepper and borax, mixed. The pepper gave a little flavor but mainly this mixture was to keep flies from laying eggs on the meat if the weather turned warm for a few days.

The meat was hung up on rafters in the smokehouse using

coat hangers straightened, then doubled over and threaded through the holes cut behind the Achilles tendon on the back of the hind leg on the hams. This was where the heavy stick with points on each end had been inserted to hold the carcass up while the hog was gutted. Uncle Page just stuck his big pocketknife through the shoulders and middlin's to make slits for the wire. The wire was then wrapped around nails on the rafters in the smokehouse to hang freely.

The smokehouse had a dirt floor. The meat would be smoked by building a small fire near the center of the room right on the dirt, using green wood. You wanted a lot of smoke, but not a lot of heat. There was a door on the smokehouse that was closed, but the building was not made to be airtight. Smoke could be seen wafting from the cracks, as if the building itself was on fire. Uncle Page usually smoked them like this for two days, waited a week and did it again for two more days. One final week's wait and they were finished off with yet a third smoking.

He wanted to go to Kenbridge and get some hickory chips from the ax handle factory to do the smoking with and he had several bushels of wheat that needed to be ground at the Kenbridge Mill, most likely wheat that he had been traded for "services rendered" in livestock of some kind. We loaded his truck, and Uncle Bo and I rode to Kenbridge with him.

Some folks called the Kenbridge Road the "Steel Bridge Road." The old, rusted steel bridge was always fun to drive. Its arched span crossed the Meherrin River in the valley between two steep hills thickly covered in hardwood trees. This section of river was as close to any true "rapids" as we had around. Deep under the riverbed and jutting just above it in several places was a huge rock bed, and the water usually exploded in a white froth as it hit and flowed over these worn and weathered rocks. Today, as on most days, the Meherrin was muddy.

Up the steep hill we went, past cattle ranches, Black Angus grazing in the lush pastures, and rolling hills. There were two old, long-ago-closed country stores on the way, and Grandaddy Gholson, my Momma's Daddy, had run them both years ago. Both had faded signs like "Nehi Soda," "Beechnut Chewing Tobacco," and "Flying A Gasoline" still nailed to the sides of the weed-choked, shuttered buildings.

I liked Kenbridge. It was a sleepy little town, even when

compared to South Hill; the downtown usually looked closed during the week, there were so few parked cars.

The Kenbridge Mill was down a little dirt side street. A white, frame, two-story building with a wide concrete unloading dock covered by a big A-frame porch. Supporting the porch were several old worn and faded pilings. The spots where the branches had been removed by ax had just worn smooth over the years but you could see where each and every limb had been. A block and tackle dangled beside a second-story door on the front side. This was used to winch up the grain to the loft area to begin the slow trickle through the grinding stones.

This mill's grinding wheels were turned by electricity and not water. Still it was a slow, laborious process. There was a slow, steady turning of stone against stone, and the grain running through made a low "grnnnnch, squeak, grnnnnch" as the wheels, now showing a little wobble from years of use, slowly turned and transformed grains of wheat into the fine, silky-smooth flour filtering below. A fine, silty, white, powdered dust always hung in the air, as well as the musty smell from years of grinding corn and wheat.

You paid just two dollars, I think it was, to grind a fifty-pound bag of wheat or corn. Used to be you waited until your batch was ground and then paid them with a portion of the grain. Now, you didn't even have to wait to pay; our wheat was weighed and they would give us the "yield," or what that number of pounds of wheat would "grind out" to.

We then headed down to the ax handle factory. As Uncle Bo sat smoking a Lark cigarette, I was looking at the large metal-covered unloading dock, entertained by "coo coo cooooo," in every direction, from the hundreds of pigeons sitting on the roof's edge, enjoying the sun.

Uncle Page and his buddy who worked here soon returned. Each held a big bean-bag-looking clear plastic bag of hickory shavings. The handles here were cut on a lathe and all the wood was hickory. It was green until kiln-dried later on. This was "just what the doctor ordered" as far as what we needed for smoking meat. The shavings were not only almost free, they were perfect for producing just the right sweet, pungent hickory smoke needed for flavor and preservation.

As we headed back home, we stopped at Gold Elliott's Store for a cold Schlitz and a little candy. Gold Elliott's looked like it belonged in Texas. It was a white concrete building with a big "false front" on it like the towns in the cowboy westerns on TV, only his front was cinder blocks and not wood. Inside it was dark. An aged brown cement floor was covered in kelly green sawdust mixed with floor polish and deodorant. It gave the place a slick-looking floor shine and a kind of wintergreen scent.

It was always fun going in a different store; they almost always had a candy you had never tried. Gold Elliott's had PayDay, a candy bar with peanuts on the outside and a caramel nougat center. They were usually fantastic. I waited until a few miles down the road to eat mine and the scent hit my nose just as I chewed down on the first bite.

It was rancid but it was "too far back to worry about it today," Uncle Page said. "I'll git you a free one next time we go back."

When we got home Grandma said, "I lost another chicken last night."

Most likely a weasel or mink Uncle Page said. Weasels could be bad news; they would sometimes kill several chickens in one night. We walked down to the chicken house and he found where the "chicken thief" had burrowed in underneath the floor joist.

"I got something at home to git him," he said. "I'll fix him up tomorrow night."

Uncle Page still had some working steel traps; he kept all his tools oiled and in good shape whether he was still using them or not. I felt sure this would be the weasel's demise.

"How's the mule?"

"Ain't doing good at all," Uncle Bo said.

Tom, our mule, had steadily gone downhill after a brief rally that at first had us convinced he was going to make it. He was now down in his stall and couldn't get on his feet. It was gut wrenching to see him laying there; he would weakly raise his head; big brown eyes following your every move and then exhale a sneezy-sounding sigh and lay back down.

Waiting on the inevitable was hard on everybody; any animal after fifteen or twenty years gets to be a part of the family. I remember Uncle Page and Daddy talking about the .22 rifle was too weak a caliber and the shotgun not an option either; it would have to be a deer rifle or the pistol. What they were discussing didn't require any imagination at all. I was sickened by the fact that Tom would have to die and somehow transfixed by the fact that Uncle Page had the stomach to do this sort of thing.

I don't know which one they used. Thankfully I was at school when it all came to an end. When I got home all were gathered at the mule shed: Mr. Baisey, Uncle Page, and Uncle Bo. Dillard Baisey had his old gray Ford tractor there with a blade on the front, and they had Tom trussed up in chains attached to a single tree, a large bar with a round swivel hook on the front and two just like it on the back. This was attached to the tractor and the chains holding Tom. As they drug him over to the backside of "the hill" to his final resting place — a shallow, scooped-out natural ravine — I thought how cold and uncaring it all seemed, but it was not. It was just reality, just necessity; there was no other way to move an animal that large, I don't suppose. Tom was gone and the lifeless shell he had lived in was all that was left. They used the tractor blade and shovels to bury him. He was covered but barely by the red clay of the bank — a hoof still stuck out as if clinging on to sunlight till the end. By noon of the second day the buzzards had started to circle and were beginning to scratch him out from under the dirt. His body had been exposed as the buzzards dug and clawed. It seemed cruel what was going on, but as Grandma said, it was "jes nature takin' its course."

"Got to tell Mrs. Johnston," she said.

We only communicated with Mrs. Johnston by mail; we had no phone. I don't know if she did or not. She lived somewhere down around Norfolk or Suffolk, that was all I knew for sure. Grandma and Grandaddy had begun the sharecropping tenure with Mr. Thomas, her daddy. After he passed, she inherited the farm and they had continued the same agreement with her. Grandma wrote what sure seemed like a long letter just to be about the mule, and licked the envelope and put the five-cent stamp on it.

The mood was somber. Uncle Bo joked about some of the things Tom had done over the years: getting spooked by a snake and tearing up almost half a row of tobacco with the slide, how he would just sometimes stop and refuse to move regardless of whether you hit him with the reins or not, until he decided he "was ready to move."

It would be a long anxious wait to hear back from the letter. Anybody that says, "Don't worry about it," I thought, is usually not involved in it. Those that are ... worry.

New Buddy Coming

Nighttime, after thousands of years of evolution, is still a little on the spooky side, even in familiar surroundings.

It was somehow almost pitch black, even though the sun was now a faint orange light covering the horizon. I twisted my way slowly through the thick brush at the bottom of the hill. My ears heard things crunching and snapping that weren't there, and my eyes were constantly picking up nonexistent movement all around me. My whole body was a bundle of tightly wound nerves.

Suddenly my right foot arched skyward of its own accord from a deep, piercing pain. Instinctively I lifted it and held on, hobbling around to get my vision adjusted and survey the damage, all the while trying not to drop the old beat-up minnow bucket I was carrying. There was just a small half-inch cut with a faded blue sliver hanging from it; I had stepped on a piece of broken glass. Being barefooted has both its good and its bad, I guess. I set the bucket down, removed the glass, and smeared the cut with red mud.

I could hear the soothing sound of the water rushing over rock way before I could see the branch. A thick fog had everything socked in. When I hit the waterline, I stepped into the icy-cold water and a shiver ran up my spine: maybe from the coldness of the branch water, maybe from the large moccasins that I knew were here. But I reasoned the water would be safer than the bank. In the water the snakes would hear me coming first and scatter, but on the bank I might startle one.

About an eighth of a mile downstream I came to my destination, a deep hole in a sharp turn in the branch. It was here that Daddy as a kid while swimming had almost cut his arm in half on a broken half-gallon Mason jar that had washed downstream. The clear glass in running water was impossible to detect, and there had been an old trash dump upstream. Heavy rains continually washed rusted cans and glass down the length of the branch.

A huge sweet gum sprang from the soil right at the edge of the water here. Under the gray, gnarled roots protruding from the bank, fat minnows usually could be seen, darting far under the darkness of the bank, back to safety. The day before, in the same old upstream trash dump, I had found an old handmade minnow trap made from a long-abandoned screen door. Just a rolled-up rectangle of wire that made a can-shaped cylinder with two other smaller rectangles of wire rolled at an angle to form the shape of a funnel, which was inserted small end first into the bigger cylinder. The minnows went in the funnel and the small opening with wire protruding kept them in place. You just removed one end to pour them into the minnow bucket, along with branch water to keep them alive. The minnow bucket had an inner bucket with holes all along the center, and when lifted and lowered several times together this put new air back in the water and kept the minnows alive longer. I found the tobacco twine that I had tied the trap to the tree roots with and eased it from under the bank. Nothing there. I was intensely disappointed to find nothing in the trap, but then again, I had put nothing in it to attract minnows, a lesson I was soon to be taught.

The morning sky had taken on a sickly yellow glow, maybe from the rain the evening before, but most likely because it was a school day. All school days started with the same sickly glow, I thought. I saw movement coming toward me from up the hill and there was no mistaking who it was: none other than Old Bob. I had tried to rouse him into coming with me earlier, but all I had gotten was a heavy sigh and a you-got-to-be-crazy look out of him.

Regardless of what you called it — streak of lean or middlin' meat — its scent was thick and sweet in the chill air of early morning. Old Bob and I both yawned simultaneously, and I wiped the sleep from my eyes for yet another time. I was beginning the climb from the branch up to the barns, legs wet and cold from the knees down and covered in the beggar lice that lined the path. It would be impossible to smell middlin' meat this far away, I reasoned; maybe I just wanted some so badly, I smelled it. We hadn't had middlin' meat in weeks anyway. It was most likely all gone. Fatback or sausage was all we had eaten in quite a while.

Grandma just shook her head when I walked into the kitchen.

"I'm gonna clean up and git ready," I said, before it could be said to me.

As I filled the wash-pan from the water bucket with the dipper, I saw peeled, freshly sliced tomatoes on a saucer, and right beside it was a big plate of middlin' meat. "Ain't no way I could've smelled that so far away," I thought as I walked to the bedroom to wash up. Maybe the day was looking up after all.

Breakfast for the most part was quiet. We mostly just looked at each other and rarely spoke, except to ask for something to be passed. Maybe because the days all started so early, maybe because everyone was bone tired from the day before, maybe there was no reason at all, I randomly thought to myself. It didn't matter anyway; all that mattered was that I had a big hand-sized biscuit oozing freshly churned butter and capped with a thick slice of tomato and two crispy pieces of middlin' meat. This, I thought, to myself would be a fittin' last meal for any death row inmate.

Uncle Bo was noisily saucering his coffee when he looked up and out the screen door. "Dere's Page," he said.

"Has he got the trailer?" Grandma asked.

"Yep," Uncle Bo replied.

"Barner Jones must have found one then," she said.

"What?" I asked.

"Mawning, Mumma," I heard Uncle Page's booming voice say from the front room.

"Mawning, Page," she said.

"Gonna git you a new buddy to play with," Uncle Page said to me, laughing.

A big wad of tobacco protruded from his cheek.

How can you chew tobacco in the morning? I thought. *Heck, how can you chew it anytime?* I had tried it once and proclaimed that I would rather chew a mule turd, a proclamation that I still stand by today.

"What kind of buddy?" I quizzed.

"New mule," Grandma said.

"How much was he?" Uncle Bo asked.

"Thirty-five dollars," said Uncle Page. "Ain't no more cheap mules anymore. They are gittin' hard to come by. He's a big white. Stocky and easy going."

My gut suddenly spasmed. There was no mistaking the sound, the steady crunch of gravel growing louder and louder only meant one thing: Uncle Clyde and that damned Number 3 school bus.

Funny, I thought, as I walked out and toward the bus, *I'm more nervous now than I was in the dark of night alone on the branch.* Then I realized: At the branch I was walking into the unknown, now I was walking into the known. At the time the known was the scarier of the two. I tried to ease my mind by thinking of the new mule that would be there when I got home that afternoon. As the door swung open and I started the climb up the steps, I thought to myself, I wish I was in the Army. Ironically many years later when I was in the Army, I remember wishing I was back on that damned school bus. I didn't know what you called it, nerves or whatever, I just knew that whatever it was, I had a bad case of it.

Squirrel Time

It really exists.

Grandaddy looked like he had been in a fistfight. His nose was almost beet-red on one side and his eye was swollen partially shut and turning a blood blister-colored blue. He and Rattler, his old black-and-tan coonhound, had been squirrel hunting in the brambles and oaks on the backside of the property, near the spring-fed branch that rambled through the bottom. I had heard Rattler's "bawoooom, bawoooom" accompanied by a high-pitched squeal, the sound a dog makes when you step on his foot accidently.

When Rattler treed, he literally tried to climb the tree. He circled and raked and scratched the bark with his front claws, round and round, as he tried to keep sight of the squirrel scrambling skyward to the safety of a leaf nest or natural hollow. He had treed at an absolutely huge sweet gum that sat to itself at the edge of the forest, the self-proclaimed king of its domain. The sweet gum got its name because you can peel the bark back and use the resin just underneath it as chewing gum. This particular tree stood alone and gorged itself in pure sunlight and an almost ever-present runoff from the nearby branch, and its health showed; it was at least 100 feet high.

The leaves and gum balls had fallen but the squirrel had gone high and on the blind side of the tree as well. Grandaddy used an old trick: he threw a big rock into the thick brush on the side of the tree the squirrel was hiding on; the squirrel, reacting to the noise, quickly darted back into view on Grandaddy's side of the tree. He aimed the single barrel .12-gauge shotgun at it, but it was so straight up the gun rested too much on his collarbone. He realized the danger in this: a .12-gauge kicks with enough force to shatter a collarbone. He had only a few seconds to formulate a plan, and maybe his solution wasn't the best. He laid down on the ground, placed the old .12-gauge between his cheek and shoulder, sighted the squirrel, and fired. The end result was a dead squirrel, a black eye, and a bloody nose from the unpredicted recoil from the blast.

When Grandaddy got to the house, he washed up and got ready to clean the two squirrels he had been lucky enough to bag that afternoon. He took out his old bone-handled O'Henry pocketknife, and a worn gray whetstone about the size of a shoeshine brush that he kept in a cigar box over the ledge of the door. He put a few drops of 3-IN-ONE oil on the stone, laid it on his knee, and holding the knife at about a 45-degree angle pulled it toward him with medium pressure. Then he would decrease the angle to about 20 degrees and cut toward the stone as he pushed off in the other direction. "Squwoosh, Squwoosh." He did this rapidly about eight to ten times, and then he made the same actions up and down on the side of an old slick rat-tailed file. This would remove the tiny filings the stone had abraded off. He would always pick up a little piece of paper and slice it with the razor-sharp blade, then rub his thumb on the edge to make sure it was "just right."

Grandaddy always wet the squirrel in the big, galvanized bucket the chickens drank from so he didn't get any hair on the meat. Hair is a real mess; no one likes to see it and you can't wash it off. You have to pick it off one hair at a time with the point of a knife. He grabbed the squirrel by the front legs and back legs and stretched it out, stomach side down. He laid it on the front porch and cut in the middle of the back down toward the backbone until the skin was cut through and wide enough for him to insert a thumb under each side. He took the squirrel over to the edge of the woods, stuck a thumb under each cut and pulled in different directions until the skin came off both front legs and hind legs. He cut right at the joint where the leg bends and removed the front feet, then cut the head off with all the skin attached and tossed it. The back legs he did the same with, cut the feet at the joint and then cut the tail off with the rest of the fur attached. There were companies that bought squirrel tails; they used the hair for tying dry flies for trout, but the eight cents they paid was not worth the effort. He stuck the knife blade just under the skin midway of the stomach and cut toward the neck, then turned the knife around and cut toward the tail. The entrails he removed with his fingers and then cut the genitals off and tossed the whole works. He then washed the squirrel in clean water and cut it into six pieces: he split the ribs in half, each with a front leg, separated the two hind legs, and the backbone he cut in half.

Grandma took them from there; she washed them again in lukewarm water and put them in a soak of salt water and vinegar.

This helps to remove any gamey taste. Contrary to popular belief, squirrels are not really "gamey"; this happens just like with any other wild animal when a shot or pellet penetrates the gut or bladder. If an animal is gutted and cleaned quickly most of this taste is eliminated. Grandaddy always killed just enough to eat and no more, and they were out of the tree, cleaned, and in the pan in short order, which takes away most bad flavors.

Grandma would parboil the squirrel until it was almost come-off-the-bone tender, and then remove and drain it. She put the big cast-iron frying pan on the woodstove, added some grease, and then put in thinly sliced onions that had been cut into small chunks. As these slowly simmered she dipped the squirrel in milk and a beaten egg that had been whisked together. The squirrel was then dredged in flour that had been salted and seasoned with a little black pepper and a small bit of cayenne pepper. By now the onions were translucent, and she drained them and set them aside. The squirrel was added along with a little more grease, and it was cooked over medium heat until golden brown, and then removed. Now to the cast-iron pan she added a little flour and a pinch of salt and pepper to make a roux. As the roux thickened, she added about a cup of water, stirred it until mixed, replaced the fried squirrel, and covered it with the onions. The whole dish was then covered by a heavy cast-iron lid and the heat reduced to a bare simmer. The smell of the onions and gravy was sweet and mellow, and any idea of a squirrel being in the pan was long gone.

We feasted on navy beans with salt pork (Grandma always put a red cayenne pepper pod in hers for a little extra zing and I always floated mine in vinegar), fried potato cakes, and biscuits so flaky you could barely cut them in half without breaking them … and something in a succulent brown gravy with onions … oh yeah, squirrel!

As we sat and ate, Grandaddy told the story of the afternoon. Now that it was history it was funny, and we laughed as he talked. Squirrels, he said, follow a clock and a routine, same as we do: if you see a squirrel on a tree tonight at five o'clock, you will see him on the exact same tree at pretty close to the exact same time tomorrow night. That bit of knowledge would later lead many a squirrel to his demise.

Uncle Bo drove off to Hines Store to sit around under the big oak trees and talk crops with the old-timers who would gather there to "tell lies," as Grandaddy called it. He and I went to the old log tobacco barn down at the big oaks and loaded my toy wagon full of acorns to feed the hogs along with the usual bucket of slop. It was hard for me to feed the hogs; they were full grown and fat and full of squeal and playfulness, but the weather had already started turning cold and there was a gnawing pain in my gut and a tightening in my throat as I pondered what lay ahead for them. I had never met anyone who liked killing livestock and I was glad for that. Uncle Page did it, but not because he liked it, just because he knew someone had to do it.

"Let's go sit on the porch," Grandaddy said.

I was glad for the interruption in my train of thought, and we headed to the house. Grandma had cleared the table and had begun the slow task of boiling water on the woodstove so she could wash dishes. We were sitting on the front porch on a beautiful fall night, no bugs to bother you, the sky clear and ablaze with stars, just talking. The TV had a broken tube, and the man in town had said it would be twelve dollars to fix it. Grandaddy had said it would be next year when we sold tobacco before it could be fixed. Twelve dollars was just more than we could spend now; we had to buy fertilizer and tobacco seed in the spring and there were just too many things that might happen between now and then to risk spending twelve dollars.

Grandma came out and sat down in her rocking chair with an audible sigh; I knew she had to be worn out. This was Pappa's kind of weather, she said; you could tell she had loved her folks from the very tone of her voice.

"Yeah," Grandaddy said. "I remember."

She was fourteen when they had married, no more than just a kid, but then she had never really been a kid. I remember her telling of chores, cooking, and cleaning from as far back as she could remember, but never of playing, not once. All either of them had ever known was hard times. They were like two kids who had grown up even as they raised kids of their own.

I sat there in the darkness and wondered what was going on in their minds, what memories of hard times they carried as a load, and what dreams they had once harbored that they knew would never now come to pass. I thought of how poor we were, but mostly I thought of how lucky I was. They had sacrificed and given me things they had never had and I vowed to myself that I would make my own kids' lives better than mine had been, and I wished that somehow I could make Grandma's and Grandaddy's lives better ... maybe by just carrying on the name and making each generation's life easier than the one before it ... maybe knowing that, would help them; they sure deserved something ... I would sure like to give them something. ... For now though, all any of us had ... was hope.

The Footsteps of The Poor

of all of mankind's mystery, human born or heaven sent,
the footsteps of the poor, do they even leave a print?
is their existence only labor, no one caring where they went?
forever walking bowed and humble, without question or lament.

do they know upon their birth, their mission here upon this earth?
is there escape within their kind, can they ever have a worth?
or is this a mold that can't be broken, maybe bent but never shorn,
a yoke that is the token, of their souls leached out and worn?

do they strive in useless toil, weak and hungry, lives forlorn,
merely serving this world's labor, as one dies, another's born?
wrinkled faces, lifeless eyes, clothes filled, just skin and bone,
rarely travel from the places, shacks and rambles they called home.

never tasted of life's pleasures, struggled daily to stay alive.
their legacy cannot be measured, very little left behind
and yet their lives were void of scandal; if life has a slate, then
theirs were clean.
They did not bully or mishandle, did not mistreat and were not
mean.

just simple plain dirt people, scratching life straight from the land,
somehow labeled as the lowest of all the classes known as man.
I've known them all in my lifetime, slowly coming to its end,
and I'm happy I can say, now to you all family or friend,
I was proud to live beside you, hear your voice, hold your hand.

we shared our hardships all together, sometimes laughed and often
cried;
reunion now will just be sweeter as we meet again on the other
side.
and if the cycle just starts over, I have no qualms, I have no fears,
as long as you are with me, to give meaning to my years.

The Striproom

I know what you're thinking, but no, it is not a club in Atlanta.

It's odd, I guess, to have an attachment to a building, but the old striproom we had before the interstate came through had its charm. It was an old log building with mud-chinked walls, a dirt floor, and only one small pane glass window. Upstairs was a loft containing old farming utensils, wooden wheat scythes, rusted steel leghold traps, broken rakes and hoes, and dirt dobber nests and red wasps. If there had been a ladder that took you up there, it had fallen off years ago. You had to find finger and toe holes in between the logs and mud and "mountain" climb your way up there. As challenging as that was, the only way down was one big, long kamikaze jump onto ground packed as hard as cement.

As kids we would go in the striproom to play and pretend it was a cave. You didn't have to pretend much. The small window faced north; little light could enter. On a rainy day it was the most depressing place you can ever imagine. I felt like a Middle Ages prisoner shackled in a dungeon. The tobacco wax in the green leaves formed a dust on the outside of the cured leaf; this dust had fallen to the floor over the decades and had built up. When you entered the striproom you were overcome by the peppery, pungent smell of the tobacco from generations past and the dank, musty smell of the damp dirt floor. It was not uncommon at all to sneeze each and every trip inside.

After it was cured, we took the tobacco to the striproom, and the leaves that had been tied on the tobacco stick were now "stripped" from those same sticks. Leaves were placed in one hand and the tips of the stems put together uniformly and flat on the end. After forming a bundle that you could just barely hold comfortably, you chose the best-colored light-bronze leaf, free of insect damage or blemishes, and wrapped the bundle together with it, then tucked the stem inside to hold it together. The wrap

106

reminded me of the old timey way a woman would tie a scarve on her head, a style a lot of country folks wore. Or a better description of the bundle might be like a cornhusk doll without arms, I guess.

If the "pullers" had picked a leaf off the plant before it was ripened enough, it would not cure, and the stem would be left "green" and not the dried brown. Green stems were frowned upon at the market and would lower the price of the tobacco at auction. Most folks simply put green stems on the inside of the bundle and the "wrapper leaf" would hide them. Not Grandma. "If it ain't right, it's wrong," she would say and she would not hide one. Usually she would take the time to peel the tobacco leaf away from the stem at the top on both sides down to where it was brown and properly cured and break it off. Then and only then would she include it in the bundle. "I ain't cheatin' nobody," she would say.

Grandma had sewn together guano bags, which were plain brown hemp fertilizer bags, into a big square. This was placed on the floor and the tobacco bundles laid on it with the loose end of the leaves facing inside, the wrapped head of the bundle facing out. These would be piled in layers until they were about waist high, then loaded onto the pickup and taken to auction.

Although South Hill has always been known for having a great auction, Uncle Bo, Grandaddy, Uncle Page, and I always went to Clarksville, at the western end of the county; to Norlina, North Carolina; or to somewhere else out of town. I know now it was just for the joy of it, just to loosen up a little bit and relieve the everyday stress of life. We would always visit the liquor store and buy a pint of whiskey on the way. On the way back we would always eat at a nice restaurant. It was my favorite time of year; it was the one time when I really felt like I "was somebody."

At auction the buyers from the various tobacco companies, like Philip Morris and Winston, would come by, pick up bundles, inspect them, and bid on them, in "auction speak": fiddy dolla, fiddy dolla, fiddy one, fiddy one, fiddy two, fiddy two. The highest bid won. Your tobacco had been weighed as you drove in, and now you took your auction ticket over for your check. We usually saved all the checks until we "settled up" with Mrs. Johnson at the end of the year.

I remember going into the striproom one day with Grandma and Uncle Bo, and a big black snake was lounging stretched across the floor. As Uncle Bo reached for a hoe standing at the door to kill it, Grandma said, "Don't kill it. Black snakes eat rats and besides it's bad luck." Uncle Bo chopped at the ground beside the snake's head and it slithered off into a little hole at the base of the floor and was gone. I took a big rock and covered the hole, but I never felt comfortable in the striproom again. After that, when we went in I would walk slowly, looking everywhere. Uncle Bo, if he got the chance, would grab me from behind, yell "boo," and I would clear the floor. Everyone would get a kick out of that and laugh until one day Grandma, for whatever reason, said, "Edward, leave that chap alone." If she called you by your first name, you knew you had touched a nerve and from that day forward I was never "gooched" again.

I think the attachment I felt for the striproom may have been because of Grandaddy and the toys he crafted for us. We had nothing to play with as kids. Wooden spools from sewing machine thread that Grandma gave us or old cat's-eye marbles we had found would have been about it if not for Grandaddy.

Behind the packhouse was an elderberry bush, the wood of which has a hard outer bark and inner wood and an unusually thick pithy center. Grandaddy would cut a piece of elderberry about eight inches long, then stop by a nearby little hickory tree and cut a small, fairly thin branch of that, about ten inches long. With a sharpened stick he would take the pith out of the elderberry bush, a little at a time until it was clean and hollow from one end to the other. He then cut a small, round "button" of wood about twice the thickness of a quarter, and with his pocketknife he would drill a small hole in the center of it and place it in the end of the hollowed out elderberry bush branch. Then he patiently whittled a "plunger" out of the hickory branch, which would slide in and out of the elderberry branch, but just barely. You pointed the closed end with the hole in it at the ground, filled the chamber about half full of water and inserted the plunger. When brought back up to the horizontal position the plunger kept the water inside. When you pushed the plunger forward it would shoot a stream of water as good as any store-bought water pistol!

We also made a "pop gun," which was completely hollow from one end to the other and had a plunger. To operate it, chew a piece of newspaper, roll the piece into a ball that just barely fits inside the hollow branch, and push that ball about halfway down. Then chew another piece that was bigger and jam it into the end of the hollow branch until that ball was as tight as it could get. When the plunger was pushed forward into the open end, the wad in the other end would fly about ten feet, accompanied by a loud pop.

In tobacco curing time we would collect wet red clay, thick with flecks of shiny mica, bring it back, and roll it into balls a little bigger than the store-bought marbles. These we would then take to the tobacco barn and place them inside the barn anywhere we could fit them without their rolling off onto the floor. As the tobacco cured, the marbles dried just as if in a kiln and would shrink down to store-bought marble size.

He also whittled me a slingshot from a big "Y" we cut from a dogwood tree, finishing it off with two strips of rubber we found from a blown-out truck inner tube in the road at Hines Store. A tongue from an old shoe cut in half with holes cut into the center of each end made the pouch. All was secured together with tobacco string. I would then roll hundreds of the little clay balls for "ammunition."

We made all these things at the striproom because it was only a short walk away from the tobacco barns. When we lounged together at the barns in hammocks that Grandma had sewn from the guano bags, we always faced the striproom.

I think in a sense I felt that when they tore down the striproom they took Grandaddy away from me a second time. I now look in sadness at the northbound lane of Interstate 85 and think to myself, "Grandaddy, they buried you twice, but they will never cover you up. Not as long as I can keep your memory alive."

Armageddon

Armageddon. That was the only explanation.

The explosion was deafening, the house shook, timbers creaked, water splashed out of the kettle on the wood heater, and the mirror alternated images of ceiling and floor, ceiling and floor.

My eyes were only partially open, but open enough to see the sun shining. It wasn't a storm.

Another thunderous explosion, and I could see debris in the air down at the 'bacca (tobacco) barn.

It was the Cuban Missile Crisis. All we had heard for over a week on the news and at school was "fallout shelter," "duck and cover," "get under your desk, and put your hands on your head." We had even gone through drills, and now it had happened. I was sure of it.

My survival instincts told me to run somewhere, anywhere, but the little boy in me said, *Let's go look at it.* So we compromised. I ran, but I ran down toward the barn.

Daddy stopped me. "Don't go no closa, dey bustin' wood wid black powda."

We were always "bustin' wood"; wood was our lifeblood. It cooked our food, heated the house, boiled our water, smoked our meats, and cured the tobacco. We were always bustin' or cutting it, with an axe or hand saw. It was usually "outsides," thin strips of wood with the bark still attached that we got from the sawmill for four dollars a truckload.

But these were big logs! Grandaddy would drive a big iron wedge into each end of the log, then drive a partially hollow black powder wedge into the center. Fill it with black powder, then insert a long fuse, light it, and run like hell to get behind one of the huge white oak trees at the barn. When the fuse hit the powder, the wedge would slam through the log, splitting it in half and shooting a large stream of sand, wood chips, and black smoke in the air. It was a beautiful thing!

It was "kinder, gentler" times then. You could buy black powder, fuses, blasting caps, and even dynamite at the fertilizer store in South Hill. No paperwork, no background check. But, hey, we still had some sense in those days; none of those things were needed.

Black powder. It was magical. It took your mind off everything. There were no worries when you had black powder. It was all the things I had heard of but never seen: fireworks, the county fair ....

The County Fair

In years past Uncle Paul and Aunt Sis had always taken me "trick or treating," and this year, since I had a few dollars saved from summer berry sales, they had agreed to take me to the county fair as well. It would be my first trip to the fair, held in Chase City, Virginia, in western Mecklenburg County, and I had long anticipated this journey after listening to the kids at school describe it.

Although it had been "Fair Day" and we had the day off from school, we decided to go at night so we could see the fireworks, another first. The only fireworks I had seen were the pop crackers, sparklers, M-80s, and cherry bombs that we occasionally set off on July 4th.

From South Hill to Chase City is twenty-two miles. Just a thirty-minute drive … we had been on the road at least four days … are we there yet? I wouldn't say it, but I sure thought it: can you drive any slower? The wait was worth it, though.

My first impression was breathtaking. All the lighted rides, the sky-high Ferris wheel, carnival music blasting the air … it was electric! We headed into a dirt parking lot that looked to hold every car in the world in it. I was "chompin' at the bit" to get out and hit the midway.

Uncle Paul said we all had to "stay together" so no one got lost. As we turned onto the first aisle of games and food stalls, the scent and sound of sizzling peppers and onions and the sight of huge, smoked sausages and "double dogs" overwhelmed the senses. I decided I had to have a "double dog." I ordered just that, with mustard, onions, and peppers. And the guy just stared at me.

"Footlong is what he wants," Uncle Paul told him.

I was embarrassed. I had never seen them or heard the name *footlong*. I just knew they were twice the size of any hot dog I had ever seen so we called them "double dogs." Mine came, and it did not disappoint. It was fantastic! It did set my pocketbook back far worse than I had planned on, however. I now had to decide if I wanted to go on a ride or play a game; I didn't have money for both.

As we walked and took it all in, I saw a booth where you threw a nickel and if it landed in a plate or bowl you won the plate or bowl. There was a big, flowered bowl in the center and I knew Grandma would like that. I wanted to win it for her.

Aunt Sis said, "Just wait till we walk around it all and then if you still want to, you kin do it."

As we walked the midway the rides were enticing, especially the Ferris wheel, the Scrambler, and Tilt-a-Whirl, but I wanted that bowl.

Suddenly a booming voice said, "She'll twitch it, and twotch it, and put it right where you can watch it."

I turned to see a scantily clad lady on a small stage with a throng of men standing around it.

"Hoochee coochee show," Uncle Paul said.

Aunt Sis shot him a look, and it seemed he was ashamed he even knew what it was called. All of a sudden, our pace quickened substantially.

"We'll go look at the exhibits," Aunt Sis said, and we walked through buildings filled with paintings, birdhouses, big watermelons, pumpkins, statues and sculptures, baked goods, and canned goods, all submitted by area students and residents. Some were adorned with big red and blue ribbons; Aunt Sis said they had won prizes! As we came back outside, I noticed an icy chill in the air and I wished I had worn a jacket like Grandma had told me to do!

We made our way back to the dish game. I had $1.15 cents left. I got $1.10 worth of nickels and began my quest. My first toss went right in and my heart jumped into my throat, but the nickel flew back out as easily as it had gone in. I tried about ten more times and missed each time. Then I won a coffee cup, and a few throws later a saucer. I had two nickels left. I threw and ... nothing. Only one left. I took my time and "wished" it in the big flowered bowl, and in it went, and ever so slowly I saw it approach the top rim, hesitate slightly, and drop off.

"Way to go," the man shouted and handed me a small box with a Golden Wedding Ring in it.

I couldn't have been more devastated. I stuck it in my pocket thinking that was about the most worthless thing I could have won.

We walked around, waiting for the fireworks to begin.

It thundered and I instinctively looked up at the sky.

Boom.

Something exploded in bright blues, greens, reds, and golds, sparklers and stars flying in every direction.

"Wow," I told Aunt Sis, "the fireworks are great!"

Then *boom* again.

"Plenty more where that came from," she said.

We sat in awe and watched the rest of the show, and what a show it was. When the big finale went off I could hardly contain myself.

How do you describe this to someone, I thought.

As I climbed in the back seat I saw my reflection in the mirror. *How cool*, I thought! The fine red silt from the midway had filled every pore in my face, and with laugh lines and forehead wrinkles creasing when I smiled, I looked like an old man!

We headed home.

They took me to Grandma's house. I went in and told her about the things I had seen and done. When she asked me if I had won anything, I remembered the cup and saucer and gave them to her.

"You were mighty lucky," she said.

I turned to leave to go over to Daddy's house to sleep, and then I felt the "knot" in my pocket. "I won this too," I said.

I handed her the box, and as she opened it I could see that it was not worthless to her at all. Her eyes sparkled. She just held it for the longest time before slowly taking it from the box.

"That's mighty pretty," she said. Her voice seemed to choke a bit. "What you gonna do with that?"

She took it out and put it on her left hand. It was like it had been made to go there. Grandaddy had never been able to get her a ring when they first got married, and I guess the thought of getting one fell along the wayside over the years as the kids and bills came along. I knew then what I was "going to do with it."

"That's for you," I said and left.

As I walked to Daddy's I thought about how much happier she was with the ring than she would have ever been with the bowl. It was a perfect way to end a perfect day.

Next morning when I came over for breakfast she was standing over the stove frying fatback, and the ring was still on her finger. I went to the back bedroom and bathed for school, the water turning orange from the layers of red Virginia silt being removed.

The following day was Saturday and everybody came over, the men to go to Claude Daniels's and us to watch TV. As we sat there, a room full of kids and the womenfolk, one of the kids asked Grandma where she got her gold ring.

She smiled a big wide smile and said, "Jimmy won it for me at the fair."

You could hear the happiness in her voice, and I couldn't have been any prouder.

Someone else said, "Ain't no gold ring, probably plastic."

Grandma just looked up and glanced at them, and that conversation was forever silenced.

Because she worked so much with her hands, the gold did wear off in less than a week, but it was still a very shiny silver underneath and she was just as happy with it. As far as I know it never came off her finger. I remember Aunt Sis telling me years later that Grandma had said it had been on so long it couldn't possibly be removed, and she said that "it's just as well."

It may not have been real gold, but real gold would have made her no happier. It was a trip and a memory for us both that real gold could never buy.

Uncle Bob

Grandma, Grandaddy, Daddy, Momma, and I had taken Daddy's old car over to Uncle Bob and Aunt Rachel's house.

Mr. and Mrs. Peters, Uncle Bob's stepparents, owned a house about a mile and a half down Brickland Road, just off the Kenbridge Road. When they had moved to a new house in Kenbridge, Uncle Bob and Rachel had moved into the house on Brickland Road. Uncle Bob was the farm foreman.

The house was a white frame, two stories, sort of a cross between a Cape Cod style and the old Sears Roebuck house that you could buy; it looked like someone had cut three sides out of a square in the roof and then lifted the roof up and put windows in it. It was surrounded by big oaks, and situated way back off the tar road, down a dirt driveway with sandy tire runs separated by a grass centerline. On each side as you drove in were old peach orchards. They raised mostly grain but the gnarled old peach orchards still produced some mighty fine fruit.

In a smaller, two-room, tarpaper-covered house just down the driveway lived Robert and Lindy Macklin. Robert worked the farm and Lindy helped Mrs. Peters with meals, the wash, and everyday chores.

Uncle Bob was almost bald, with strong German features, a broad forehead, full high cheekbones, horn-rimmed glasses, and more often than not a big wide grin. He seemed to take pleasure in the simplest things, and I have never known anyone to purely enjoy food as he did. Regardless of what Aunt Rachel cooked he would eat it with great relish, licking his fingers and smacking his lips. But Aunt Rachel could cook!

Aunt Rachel was small, bigger than Grandma but with some of her features — the thin face, high cheekbones. She kept her brown hair short and curly and wore slacks as often as any dress. She was always fun, but she was like Uncle Page: she would let you know what was on her mind.

I had wished we had been going for supper because, as I said, Aunt Rachel could cook up a storm, especially pies. Pecan chess with a thick, creamy molasses center and lemon chess with a sweet, zesty lemon filling. When it came to desserts of any kind, she was as good as it got.

They had a television set that could get all four channels, the secret being an outside antenna that could be turned by a control box inside the house. Grandaddy loved to watch *Wagon Train*, the whole family did, but him especially. *Gunsmoke, Bat Masterson, The Rifleman, Sugarfoot, Cheyenne, The Lone Ranger*. Westerns were in their heyday during this time.

It was not television I was waiting for; however, I bid my time and then asked Uncle Bob if he would "show me his planes." He walked to the edge of the room near the staircase and pulled a long string with a wooden knob on the end, and out of nowhere a set of drop-down steps appeared. He ascended first into the darkness and I followed on his heels. At the top of the stairs, a tug on yet another long string brought to life the single 60-watt bulb suspended from the ceiling. Just the sight and smell of the cavernous attic beams themselves were worth the trip: wide, unvarnished planks of heart pine, liberally dotted with giant crosscut knots where the tree limbs had long ago been attached to the trunks, and the sick, sweet smell of pine rosin.

But the treat we had come to see was the "sky full" of airplane models Uncle Bob had hanging from strings, as if suspended in flight. Hawthorne was a German name and Uncle Bob was proud of all things German. The only car he would ever own had to be a Volkswagen. I sat mesmerized for hours listening to him talk of Werner Von Braun and how he had been the father of America's rocket and space programs. He was especially proud when Von Braun's 1969 Saturn V rocket took man to the moon.

He had plastic models of Messerschmitts, Wildcats, P-51 Mustangs, Hellcats, and P-61 Black Widows, all with the correct paint schemes and decals, and more importantly he could tell you minute details about them all. He always had the slotted balsa wood gliders that you slid together at precut slots. They also included a rubber band, attached to a propeller and fastened to a stationary screw at the rear. You would hold them ever so gently in one hand, and turn the propeller, which wound the rubber band until tight. Then you aimed it and released it with both hands into the air, only to have it fly away to everywhere but where you wanted it to go. Somehow, he always had an "extra" that he didn't need, for me to take home.

Uncle Bob loved sheep stew, and the best in the world is made fairly close by, in Dundas, Virginia. They simply call it "cush" there. It is just like the original Brunswick Stew, made and named in 1828, only the squirrel is replaced by sheep. It takes twelve hours to cook the culled sheep in four eighty-gallon cast-iron pots and requires five shifts and up to twenty men. On occasion Uncle Bob would get a hankering for some and he and Robert Macklin would cook their own in a big cast-iron cook pot, but even Uncle Bob agreed, the best is made in Dundas. I never acquired a taste for it; it was just a little too greasy for me.

He had gone to VPI (Virginia Polytechnic Institute and State University, now simply Virginia Tech) and he was, and still is, in my mind one of the most intelligent people I have ever known. What endeared him to me even more was that he would talk to you — whether a young kid or a grown man — as an intellectual equal. He talked to me like I was a man, and I liked that. He inspired more self-reflection and deep thought in me than any teacher was ever able to bring to the surface.

Uncle Bob took me fishing in Llewellyn Barnes's farm ponds and taught me to catch bream on the bed. When bream are bedding they won't eat, but they won't tolerate anything in the beds they scoop from the pond bottom either, and that is their undoing. We would put on sunglasses to see through the water better, pick out a fat bream on a bed, and plot his demise. Putting a fat red wiggler on a hook, you cast it just beyond the bream bed, then by "fingering" the line you edged it ever closer until it slid down into the conical-shaped bed and rested on the bottom. The skittish bream would fly out of the bed. All you had to do then was sit down so your presence was not visible to the bream and watch your line; in just a minute or so you would see it begin to move and tighten as the bream picked the worm up in his mouth, not to eat it, but to clean it from his bed. It was then you would set the hook and what a fight they put up. These were slab-sized bream, bigger than a man's hand and so thick you could barely hold them to take them off the hook.

When we cleaned the bream we would make a cut just about a half-inch deep, starting at the head and working back to the tail, just along the big top fin. Grandma would fry them in hot grease, battered in fine cornmeal, pepper, and salt. Where you had made the cut the flesh would "curl" when cooked. You grab the curl and pull and all the meat slides off in a fine-flaked slab, sweet and juicy as the finest flounder, and the pesky small bones stay put. If you have ever gotten a fish bone caught in your throat, you know just how important that is. You ate the crusty cooked fins as well and what was left looked like the cartoon fish on TV.

We also went "shadding" on the Tar River, in North Carolina. Uncle Bob and Uncle Page both had giant shad nets, which looked like Paul Bunyan's tennis rackets — eight- to ten-foot-long handles with a big, deep net. We would sit on special wooden platforms that had been built on the river years ago, and with the water flowing upstream wait until a school of shad, sometimes eight or ten at the time, swam into the net. It was all the two of us could do to lift them at times. He could tell the buck or male shad from the female roe shad, and the latter were returned to the water.

Shad are too bony to eat unless slow cooked, on a woodstove, when the bones will dissolve. Grandma would remove the membrane from the big orange or yellow roe sacks and fry them to a golden brown to be served with eggs for breakfast or a quick dinner as well.

What I didn't understand as a child was the true richness of a close-knit family, the sheer treasure of a shared experience, the timeless bond that was formed by everyday occurrences. Uncle Bob passed away far too early; I think he was only fifty-two. I have grown to realize that as we age, Death somehow evolves with us, its meaning ever changing, with each passing. His memory is fresh in my mind, but like the others before him, and the ones who would follow, I knew he had taken a small piece of my heart that can never be replaced.

Uncle Bo

Uncle Bo evidently took more off Grandma's side of the family. He did not have the "Reese belly," was thin like her, and was very quiet and introverted, unlike Uncle Page and Daddy. Uncle Bo had receding, thinning dark hair, which he kept in a "buzz cut" about a quarter-inch long, and long sideburns that looked like a big cowboy boot turned sideways but always kept those close cropped as well. His face wrinkled early on and combined with his slow, patient gait made him look older than he was. Unlike Uncle Page he avoided confrontations and was more prone to tell someone what he thought they wanted to hear. I don't mean he would lie; he just made whatever he said come across as easily as it could be said. He constantly smoked Lark cigarettes, with the activated charcoal filter, as the commercials touted.

He was a very quiet man. The only way you would engage in any conversation with him was to ask him a question, and if that question could be answered with a "Yeah" or "Naw" that would be all you got. Grandma and Uncle Bo would talk and carry on conversations, but then again, we're talking Grandma. I'm convinced that whoever coined the expression "You can't get blood from a turnip" had never given Grandma the chance to try it.

He rarely showed emotion of any kind. I had seen the mule make him mad a time or two but never folks. And he had a lot of patience with kids, I noticed. Uncle Bo had never been married but he loved to play and tease and talk to babies and small kids. He didn't like to hold them, but if someone else had them, he seemed to have a good time messing with young'uns. I always thought he would have made someone a good daddy.

Uncle Bo, like the others, had a limited education, but he was very good with engines, be they small lawnmower engines or car and truck engines. He never used a mechanic; anytime his vehicles broke down he simply tinkered with them until he could fix them himself. He was also good at math; he would help me with math problems I had for school homework, all the way through Algebra 1. When I hit Algebra 2, God help us, we were like the two fish that swam into a concrete wall and said "dam."

Uncle Bo constantly invented things from junk we had lying around. He got running two old lawnmower engines someone had given him. And with just spare washers, nuts, pieces of pipe, and hoses he found at junk piles around the area, he fashioned a pump to water the plant bed and a sprayer for the MH-30 we put on the tobacco from them.

The plant bed was a big square of finely tilled soil surrounded by four logs into which the tobacco seeds mixed in with a little fertilizer were broadcast by hand. Then a very thin, white, loosely woven "bacca cloth," as they called it, was attached to the log poles with barbed wire nails — a big horseshoe nail used to attach barbed wire to fenceposts. This kept harmful insects and birds off the emerging plants. Uncle Bo ran a pipe down into a small hole where he had partially dammed the branch; the old lawnmower engine pulled water up into a sprayer head he had mounted to a tobacco stick and we watered on an as-needed basis.

The tobacco grew in this patch until it was about eight inches tall and big enough to be transplanted by hand, one plant at a time, with a tobacco planter. Grandma, Uncle Bo, and Aunt Sis would gently pull the plants and place them in wooden-handled peach baskets with the root ends touching a wet rag placed in the bottom. The tobacco planter was a long V-shaped tube of rolled tin with a "jaw" on the bottom end that was the pointed part of the "V." This jaw opened and shut when you pulled on the handle at the top end, releasing the inserted tobacco plant down a tapered round chute at the front. A small amount of poisoned water from a reservoir separated by a thin wall flowed from the chute into the hole formed when you jammed the planter into the hilled rows. This was to kill nematodes and nourish the plant as it began its journey toward harvest.

Uncle Bo rigged a sprayer from one of the engines and fashioned a more stable wooden slide that could be pulled by the mule.

In this tedious manner we moved about twenty-four inches at a time over the three fields totaling about four acres. When I complained, Grandma gently reminded me that in her day it was done with a sharpened, thick, tapered stick called a peg and you stayed bent over the entire time, as did the water boy hand pouring a small amount of water in each hole.

It took a minimum of three people to plant the way we did:

one to work the planter, one to drop the plants into the chute, and one to tote the water. The planter was filled with water mixed with MH-30, carried bucket by bucket from a fifty-five-gallon drum pulled on a wooden slide by the mule. Although labeled "Poison," MH-30 carried no warning labels like products today. With an old rag we would go down each row, dipping the rag in poison and letting it trickle down the tobacco plants, all done bare-handed. You would dip your hand in poisoned water for hours at a time and if someone went to the store for a drink and cookie, hands were never washed. You stayed in the field.

We also used it as an herbicide to keep suckers off the tobacco. Suckers were smaller bunches of tobacco leaves that tried to grow between the stalk of the tobacco plant and the primary or larger leaves. If left alone they would stunt the growth of the primary leaves, resulting in a loss of income. They had to be removed by "suckering" and that was a time-consuming, tedious job hated by all.

MH-30 had a reeking smell that permeated everything it touched; nothing was immune. Even metal, days afterward, smelled like it too had been poisoned by the stuff.

MH-30 was lethal and was eventually taken off the market. Uncle Bo died at age fifty-four, and I'm convinced it was the MH-30 that caused his early death.

Our tractor was named "Old Tom," a big powerful dark black mule, well-mannered and easy-tempered. He ate mostly what he could forage from the pasture and a little hay and corn if he was very lucky. Many times I have seen Uncle Bo riding on the back of the slide carefully guiding the mule down the tobacco rows, with the MH-30 spraying on the tobacco and him evenly. He would be wringing wet with poisoned water when it was all done. Bathing was done simply with a washrag, a bar of soap, and a small hand-carried wash-pan, so I feel sure much poison residue remained. Old Tom died at an early age also, and I'm sure it was MH-30 that did him in as well.

I saw Uncle Bo from time to time after I left home but he had little to say, as always. I was no longer living there and sometimes I felt like I was an outsider now.

He met a lady and dated and eventually said they were

married. He moved away from Grandma's, into her house. She had a small house, or double-wide trailer, on Lake Gaston. Aunt Rachel said that the two of them acted like teenagers, holding hands and walking around the farm. They went to Busch Gardens in Williamsburg on their "honeymoon" and I'm sure that must have been a treat for him, since he had never been anywhere that I knew of. He rarely even went to tobacco auctions out of town.

The story does not have the fairy-tale ending I would like to be able to tell you. But it did have a happy ending of a different kind.

The lady Uncle Bo was married to had some kids from a previous marriage who decided to "return home," maybe because of a hardship, I'm not sure. She told Uncle Bo he would have to leave and go back to Grandma's house until they left. They never did leave.

He was very depressed after returning home. There was no tobacco and his only income was from one hour a day when he worked at Hines Store while Ray Hines went home for lunch and some occasional Sunday work there. Then his health failed: his stomach started to swell and he was diagnosed with colon cancer and given two months to live. I learned that on a call I made back home one day to Aunt Sis, and I remember I wondered what I would say to him when I got to see him again, how I would handle it. I never got the chance; he died while still in the hospital, about two weeks later. I happened to call Aunt Sis that day to see how he was doing, and her daughter Wanda answered the phone and said he had passed. She said he had told Uncle Page's daughter Carolyn, who was there on a visit that afternoon, "It must be time. Can you see that?" then pointed at the ceiling, and told her, "I can see the sky opening up." And he passed.

Another link in the chain of the family had fallen away but the rest was still strong. Grandma was still there. And she paid for his funeral. The lady to whom he had been married came to the funeral home and told Grandma she wanted to see him "put away better" than in the casket Grandma had picked out for him, and told her she would help pay for it. Grandma reluctantly agreed … and the lady was never seen or heard from again. Grandma was left to pay the entire bill; I think around five thousand dollars. Grandma would always silence anyone who brought that up and say, "You don't know what troubles she may have had herself. Best just to leave it lay."

A Good Day in The Neighborhood

Grandaddy owned an old open-faced bait-casting fishing reel, and Uncle Bo and Uncle Page had an old Zebco 202, but for the most part we were a family of cane poles. Frank Rogers and his wife, Teet, who owned the farm and house Uncle Page lived in, had a big "bamboo grove" in front of their house, right at the road's edge. Although some folks would just stop and outright cut one and then drive off, we always asked if it would be okay first.

I don't remember what Mr. and Mrs. Rogers looked like. Daddy always went to the back door. The old house seemed mysterious, two stories with a tin roof and made of old weatherboard that had long ago lost its paint, if it indeed had ever been painted. The trees and bamboo hid most of the house from the road except for the long covered porch that ran along the side. You could see the white porcelain water bucket and dipper, the well with its bucket and chain, and little more. Uncle Page had always said they were good people; they just stayed to themselves. You seldom even saw them at Hines Store. Mrs. Rogers canned almost everything they ate; often you would see jars of canned food cooling on the porch rail. A product of the Great Depression, Mr. Rogers was known to "squeeze his nickels."

Seems like we were always fishing. Grandaddy and Mr. Baisey, up at the dam or Roanoke River, in one of the many creeks that Buggs Island Lake had captured during its filling, or at my favorite place: Lake Gordon. Grandaddy liked to fish for bigger fish — catfish, carp, and bass — and Lake Gordon, a long, narrow, finger-shaped lake, situated in a picturesque rural valley, had the biggest of them all — muskellunge!

The sign where they would put the johnboat in at the small weed-choked boat landing said, "Minimum Keep Size for Muskellunge 24 Inches." To the left of the boat landing was the dam and the water lazily cascaded into a big natural rock pool some fifteen feet below, before continuing its march in the deep, rock-strewn creek to the Roanoke River. The rock pool was also a great place to fish, but only after a heavy rain had deposited a load of unsuspecting fish from the lake.

I had been with them only a couple of times and we had never caught one of the "big 'uns," but they told stories of fish up to four feet long coming off the lake. The stories were not hard to believe. Lake Gordon had been left in a natural state during its construction in 1949. Stumps from logged trees dotted the lake floor. The banks and shallows were chock-full of thick aquatic vegetation, bulrushes, lilypads, cattails, and vines of all description. Lurking in the black water and routinely caught were citation-sized bass, twenty-two inches long and more than eight pounds in weight. And huge, eleven-inch-long redear sunfish and eight-inch-long bluegill would wallow in the shallows during the spring spawn.

The early mornings were always an orgy of senses: the pungent smell of spawning bream and sunfish; the eerie feel of the boat suddenly stopping in the semidarkness and creaking and scraping as you "rocked" it to clear the top of a stump or submerged log; the sight of white heron and sandhill cranes standing like statues, one leg raised and ankle deep in the shallows; and the booming sound of a "thwooooshhh" as a bass or pickerel burst the surface in a frenzy of topwater feeding, the droplets of the splash falling gently back, like rivulets of pearls, into the dark water. Lake Gordon is pocked with lush coves, steep sloping sides leading to deep, narrow pools that corral big catfish and carp. A day on Lake Gordon even without a bite is still a memory in itself.

Uncle Bo liked to river fish, mainly at Dixie's Bridge, where the creek entered into the river. He often caught large channel catfish and his favorite fish, redhorse, out of the deep hole dug out by the swirling waters after a heavy rain, when the two churning bodies of water hit head on. Like us, he mainly bottom fished, a dough-ball or fat gob of red wigglers dangling about twelve inches below a thick lead sinker. Some folks used chicken livers, but Grandma preferred to cook ours in the grease left by thin pieces of streak of lean in the thick cast-iron frying pan.

"Why use something to fish with that tastes better than anything you will catch?" she would laugh.

Sundays would often find us at Elderberry Rock, before the interstate forever severed it from vehicular traffic; after that Melvin Gill no longer allowed you on the property because he had fenced it in for cattle pasture. Elderberry Rock was just a fun place; it was more than a mile off the main road, down what was little more than a logging trail and if there had been any rain at all, we usually parked and walked. It had its charm, spring or fall. The thick hardwoods were vibrant with a patchwork quilt of color in the fall, and the wildflowers, cow itch vine, honeysuckle, and dandelion teased not only your eyes with their majesty but also your nose with the thick, sweet scents of spring. The end of the path descended into thick beech trees, with a clean forest floor of decayed leaves and dried black silt, deposited by the rise and fall of the river. We, as others before us, had long ago carved our names into the huge old-growth beech trees, and the initials just got bigger and plainer as they scarred over, year after year.

The river had two deep holes just in front of the rock outcroppings. The water was usually a deep bluish-black and almost always good fishing, especially if rain had swollen the river, since it would continually drain new fish into the holes. The grown-ups bottom fished, using red wigglers if the water was clear and dough-balls if muddy, because in the muddy, running water a fish had to rely on scent more than sight and the dough-balls with the heavy vanilla flavoring gave off a double attractant, both scent and a sweet slime. I lacked their patience and liked to fish with my cane pole, a round red-and-white bobber about three feet up and "enough worms to choke a horse," as Grandaddy used to tease me.

As we fished, we would sit on the rock soaking up the warm rays of the sun and eat Vienna sausages, sardines, Georgia hash, and potted meat straight from the can with wooden ice cream spoons. Small packs of saltine crackers would be passed around as would be vinegar, which we sometimes took in small blue Alka-Seltzer bottles, to spice up the vienna sausages and sardines. Usually I had an Orange or Grape Tru-Ade and the men, Schlitz or Pabst Blue Ribbon.

The night's supper would be twirling and glistening in the water below, secured into the bank by the sharp metal spike of the fish stringer. Grandma always had a backup pot of navy beans and potato soup ready to go, along with fresh, fried hoecakes just in case we came home empty-handed, which we often did. It was a win-win situation as far as I was concerned.

If nothing was biting, I quickly became bored and just wandered the woods after being told to watch out for copperheads and water moccasins, both of which were far more plentiful than the fish here.

Daddy, Grandaddy, Uncle Page, and I had piled into his old '58 Ford pickup truck. I sat in the back in the bed, wind in my hair, my favorite riding spot of all! We were driving down an old rutted, grassed-over logging road off Highway 1 near the Roanoke River, headed for the mouth of Robbins Creek. It had rained a few days earlier and we were hoping the water wouldn't be too muddy. This was a good spot, but few folks fished it because few even knew it existed and the ones that did, usually didn't try to negotiate the road in. We got there, parked, and began the foot journey, almost a half-mile long, through a worn-out footpath, poison oak, sumac, and cattails, bordered by thick reeds and rush.

Uncle Page told of how when they were kids they would cut cattails and Grandaddy would take a jug of kerosene, dip the cattails in the kerosene, and light the soaked cattails, to use as torches to fish by and to find their way back to the truck with. Grandaddy said that when fully soaked, they would burn for hours at a time.

Grandaddy carried an old fruitcake tin, with potato cakes, hoecakes, and fried slices of fatback wrapped in wax paper. A paper sack with a garden tomato for each of us, to peel, load with salt, and eat like an apple would finish off the meal. We had a large Mason jar of ice water, as well as a pint Mason jar also filled with a clear liquid: moonshine.

We arrived at a big circular cove where the creek entered a sharp bend. The overhead canopy was thick with willow and sweet gum trees. The water had just a tinge of color.

"Perfect," Grandaddy said, "just dark enough to hide the hook."

After arriving, while they surveyed the situation, they each took a long, measured swig from the small jar, followed quickly by "ahhhhhhh," as if it sho nuff was good! Then they baited up with some vanilla-flavored dough-balls Grandma had made for catfish. I threaded a big red wiggler on my hook and eased the line from the cane pole under an overhanging branch on the water's edge and almost immediately, zzzzzzing, the line cut through the water and I set the hook. It was heavy and it didn't want to leave the safety of the water.

"Pull him out quick, 'fore you spook the hole," Uncle Page

said.

Into the sunlight came a fat shellcracker, the yellow of its belly and fluorescent blues and reds of its gills on fire in the morning sun. Almost in tandem Daddy pulled a hand-sized bluegill from the water's edge on the other side. Grandaddy hauled in a catfish close to two pounds in size just a minute or so later. Uncle Page was "skunked" so far. He eventually caught up and in about an hour we had a loaded stringer and were about ready to go.

Uncle Page placed his rod on a waist-high Y-shaped rod holder he had fashioned with his pocketknife from a sweet gum branch and jammed into the creek bank. He grabbed the "shine" from the cool water, shook off the excess moisture, removed the lid, and said, "No use taking a chance on this spoiling" and laughed. He took a swallow, and Daddy and Grandaddy went over to finish it off.

"Betta not forget to take yo momma's jar back," Grandaddy warned.

"Damn," Uncle Page shouted as his rod bent almost double.

We all laid down our poles since this was the "bigun" for sure. The fight lasted longer than my attention span, and I started rolling mud marbles on the woods' edge. I looked up to see Uncle Page with a soft drink bottle raised over his head, then he brought it down in a resounding "thwaaack" against something. I ran over to see. I thought it was an alligator; it was almost three feet long, had a long thin mouth, and rows of razor sharp teeth.

"Gar," Uncle Page said, "ain't good for nothing but hurting somebody." He removed the hook and slid the fish back into the water with his foot. "Just dazed him enough to get my hook," he said.

The gar groggily kicked itself off, leveled out, and headed back into the depths with a few swishes of its large tail fin. It was time to go. Grandaddy's line and the dough-ball had been in the water, the rod just lying on the bank, wedged down with a Y-shaped stick, the two prongs pushed in the mud just ahead of the reel to anchor it. As he picked it up and began to wind the line in, the end bowed heavily.

"Hooked on a log," he said. "It broke loose but it's heavy, and hard to reel."

Every so often as he alternated lifting and lowering the rod to wind the line in, he would comment, "It almost seems to be moving."

They saw each other about the same time, a giant snapping turtle, its jaw with a hook in it, and Grandaddy. He reacted by instinct, I guess, and with one hand held the rod and with the other grabbed its back leg and pulled it onto the bank. The resulting low-pitched scream sounded so painful it hurt me.

"Bit me," he hollered.

I was immediately horrified, because I had heard Grandaddy say if a turtle bit you, it "wouldn't let go till it thundered."

Uncle Page grabbed the rod and Grandaddy wrapped his bleeding thumb in his blue bandanna handkerchief. He had been lucky; the turtle had taken a triangular patch of top skin mainly just between his right thumb and index finger and had bitten slightly into the "web" there.

It was an alligator snapping turtle. The inside of their mouth and cheeks is dark and they have a pink worm-like appendage growing from their tongue. They lie on the bottom and extend the tongue, wiggling this "fake worm," and then eat the unsuspecting fish that come to feast on the "worm." Because they eat fish, the meat, which is both white and dark like chicken meat, sometimes has a fishy taste. They are, however, omnivorous and will eat just about anything.

We loaded up the fish, jars, and trash, and Daddy and Uncle Page each grabbed a back leg and toted the turtle slowly to the truck being ever so careful of the snapping jaws of its thick head. It was close to thirty pounds, I would guess.

Grandaddy took the turtle home and put him in a big fifty-five-gallon barrel and fed him table scraps of vegetables and pork to "clean him out." After a few weeks of "cleansing" he was then ready to meet the axe and the same fate as the chickens. Grandaddy put a big stick down into the barrel and the turtle snapped down on it. Grandaddy then lifted him out with the stick and placed his outstretched head on the chopping block. The turtle never let go, even when his head was severed by the axe.

The shell was removed and used as a container to hold water for the chickens, I guess kept for the same reason you keep deer horns, to relive the memory. The turtle was sectioned much like a chicken. Grandma skinned him and soaked the pieces in vinegar and salt water overnight, and then seasoned, battered, and fried him in the cast-iron skillet. None of us, including her, would eat turtle; it was just too "fishy" tasting, so we invited Mr. Baisey over. He always never missed a meal of turtle or groundhog, something else only the two of them would eat.

The night after fishing at Elderberry Rock, as we rode to Oakwood Cemetery to visit family graves, which we would often do, we slowly made our way through town and past the houses along Mecklenburg Avenue, the main drag. I wondered what other folks might be doing right about then. I somehow felt sure that there was both good and bad days for everyone ... regardless of where you lived or what you did ... this one had sure been good to me!

Saturday Morning

Saturdays somehow always seemed to be special days and continue to be so right on up till today. If we made a "trip into town," it was almost always on Saturday morning. During the week I would have to be reminded, cajoled, sometimes even threatened before I would grab the wash-pan, put a few dippers of cold water in it, grab the Lux bar soap and a worn-to-a-frazzle, but clean, wash rag, and head off to an unoccupied bedroom to take what some folks call a "bird bath." (Some folks called them "wash cloth" but we called 'em "wash rag" and with good reason, I thought.) I would stop by the woodstove on the way and pour some hot water from Grandma's old cast-iron kettle into the pan to warm it up a tad.

But on Saturdays, if we were going to town, I was clean, my nice clothes on, ears washed, hair slicked down, and sitting at the table with feet and legs twitching, waiting on everyone else to get ready. Weekdays Grandma would sometimes have to "throw the covers off me" to get me up. I give you my word, in the cold Southside Virginia winter, when it's about twelve degrees outside and you are asleep in an unheated bedroom and someone throws the cover off you, you WILL wake up and get up rather quickly. You may be in need of a defibrillator, but you will be up!

Grandma would always have on her best homemade dress, pressed and starched, knee-high stockings, and a faux pearl necklace. Uncle Bo would have a starched work shirt — Saturday's was usually tan — and pressed "carpenter overalls," with the loop on the side where the hammer went. He saved the tan shirt for the weekend because it "showed dirt" too easily and you couldn't wear it in the fields during the workweek.

I laugh now, but we would usually be gone before 7:30 a.m. so we could "beat the crowd." I had always wanted to see this mysterious "crowd." I visualized South Hill as being full of folks like it was for the Harvest Festival Parade or the Christmas Parade but I had never seen it like that on a Saturday. Then again that's why we left early, so we could get a good park.

Uncle Bo had an old black '61 Ford with the winged fins, starting at the edge of the back door and extending in a C-shaped curl all the way to the back bumper. From behind, the car looked like it had a handlebar mustache. Grandma would ride shotgun and I sat in the backseat. Grandma would always wave at "Old Man Conner" who would already be out and sitting under the walnut tree, fresh coffee steaming from his cup on the old wire spool table. Just ahead would be the stop sign and the Kenbridge Road, and as we turned left I could see Uncle Paul's black Vauxhall sitting in the yard and I knew he and Aunt Sis were still at home; they usually went to town on Saturdays also.

We would drive slowly, looking at the 'bacca fields and crops along the way. If there was more than one car in the lot at Mr. McKinley's store someone would comment, "Badeye got a crowd this morning." Somehow I was getting the feeling it didn't take very many people to make what they called a "crowd."

We'd turn right and about a mile and a half later the road would take a sharp left at Claude Daniels's store. The parking lot would almost always have several cars.

"Some folks starting a little early today," Uncle Bo would say.

You couldn't start selling beer until seven a.m. but there would always be a few thirsty souls waiting for the door to open.

"Need a little hair of the dog to git over last night," Uncle Bo would mumble.

I didn't know what that was either, even though I'd specifically heard Daddy tell Claude Daniels on occasion, "Claude, I need a little hair of the dog." I was aware, that whatever it was, they put it in the beer, because that's all I ever saw Claude hand Daddy back.

We continued on past the old Pepsi-Cola Bottling Plant, G&V Amoco, and then into the heart of the "city"! The A&P Supermarket was on the right, where Grandma would shortly be buying her Eight O'Clock Coffee that she used in the percolator. In the summer, when money got tight, she would switch back to Luzianne coffee with chicory because it was much cheaper.

We usually got caught by the "stoplight." Yes, *the* stoplight; there was just the one. Montgomery Drug was on our left and Garland Drug on our right. The two stores took turns being open on Sunday so the town would always have a drugstore open if one was needed. Down the hill, past Jeffreys-Lambert Hardware and then by W.H. Crowder & Sons Department Store, both on the right. Usually I could see Mr. Crowder sitting on a stool behind the horseshoe-shaped glass display cases, reading the *Richmond Times-Dispatch*, and Daddy leaning on the case, cigarette in hand, smoke lazily drifting upward.

Uncle Bo would usually go just beyond the railroad tracks and if no car was coming make a wide looping U-turn and park in front of the depot, the old train station. Grandma would get out, cross the side street, past Crews Funeral Home, and head on uphill to Hines Supermarket, her first stop. Uncle Bo usually just sat in the car; he liked to watch the traffic go by. When I looked back he would have his left arm lazily hanging out the window, smoke faintly drifting from the cigarette cradled gently in his lips.

I headed over to Crowder's, my first stop. After a "good morning" to everyone, I would finish the "Jumble" in the paper; they always had one or two words figured out and inked in but never more.

"Can I have a dime?" would be my next question and aimed at Daddy.

"What did you do with Momma's dime?" he would always ask. Grandma always gave me a dime on Saturday mornings.

"I have it," I would say and produce it for him to see.

"Save your money and spend mine," he would chuckle and dig in his pocket for a dime.

Immediately I would go to the big Coke machine at the back of the store. The small bottles of Coca-Cola were all it held. You put in your dime and pushed down on a handle. The big round drum in the center holding the soft drinks would "whrrrrrrrrrr" and with the startling "cliiiiink" of glass hitting metal, a Coke would magically pop out of the square hole in the bottom. They were always just above freezing and sometimes even had ice in them. I always got a headache and had to stop for a few minutes because I drank too fast.

I was then out and on the street. It was funny; I would sometimes run into a kid who wouldn't give me the time of day in school, and yet on a Saturday, alone on the sidewalk, they would always say "hello" or "good morning." I guess Saturdays just put everyone in a better frame of mind.

Now I had a decision to make: snow cone or a toy from the dime store? We had no less than three five-and-ten-cent stores, and a dime would buy a lot.

Like Japanese handcuffs, a long, woven, wooden mesh tube. You put a finger in each end and pulled and you were "caught"; you had to push back inward to release yourself. Nah; I would just do that once and put it back in the bin.

I already had jacks and marbles. We had an old deck of cards. Toy cars were twenty-five cents so that was out of my league. I had a rubber ball. You could buy an Indian headdress with fourteen real feathers in it, but they were pink and yellow and blue and didn't feel very "Indian."

Today I decided on a spinning top; it was made of wood and looked like someone had cut the tapered end off the bedpost and driven a nail in it backwards, with the pointed end out. It came with a string that you wound around it, looped the circular tied opening over your index finger. Then you threw it kind of sidearm style and it would spin for almost a full minute at a time, before wobbling and falling over. This would turn out to be a bad choice because the only solid and not slatted wooden floor we had was in Grandma's house and I couldn't do it there because she was afraid I would break something.

Almost instinctively I headed back to Uncle Bo and the car. It was good timing; Grandma was coming down the sidewalk and a "bag boy" was carrying her two sacks of groceries. She would always tip him a dime after he put them in the back seat. The trip home would usually be just a simple back and forth about who Uncle Bo had seen ride by or who Grandma had run into at the grocery store.

I always waited in the kitchen because I enjoyed seeing the "sacks" emptied. In tobacco season Grandma sometimes got "store-bought biscuits" in the can because you could get a four pack of biscuits with six biscuits in each can for twenty-four cents and they saved her time in the early morning. Usually, though, it was just washing powder, dish detergent, oatmeal, and bar soap. I always eagerly awaited the sight of a coconut because I knew what that would mean.

I would then change back into my old clothes, and Grandma always commented without fail, "The day is half gone and I ain't done nothing."

Usually I would grab something to eat so I had lunch "over with." Then I'd go find the pitchfork and an old tin can, go to the mule shed, dig some red wigglers, grab my cane pole, and head off up to the pond and "the big one." The bream always cooperated and occasionally a "keeping-size" bass; they better be more than fourteen inches long like the "Game Book" said or you better not bring them home. I don't even have to tell you whose rule that was.

These memories were somehow brought back to life by an email from a friend this morning. She had commented on feeling sad during the snow because her mom had recently passed away and her mom had loved the snow. Everyone who has lost a friend or family member knows what it is like when your memory of them is jogged by a sight or sound or smell. It used to make me sad, but then I thought, maybe that is when they are the closest to me somehow, and I grew to where I welcomed those times.

Afterward as I sat there it occurred to me: we are all still interconnected somehow — family and childhood friends — we share a bond, unshattered by the passing of time, distance, or circumstance. A tiny yet still flickering ember that can be brought back to life, simply by sharing a laugh or a memory. Whether by design or by coincidence, there are few things that life has to offer that are truly better. The trick is to not become so hardened by the trials and tribulations of everyday life that we are unable to reach our heart back across time, because as surely as there is a sun and a sky, there is a heart from the past waiting, and in some cases needing, to hear from us, often only us.

Uncle Page

Uncle Page was a large man, with a bit of a belly. Seems like a Reese trait; everyone from Grandaddy on down had "six pack abs," which did not have the same connotation they carry today. He had a dimple in his chin and permanent laugh lines, traits that I am proud to possess as well. A rugged, well-tanned, strong-looking demeanor, with steely, piercing eyes. In his younger years he would have made a good model for a Marine recruiting poster; he projected toughness. His hands were big, thickly calloused, and scarred, and once he had a hold of something, he was like a snapping turtle. There was no "let go"; you just had to pray he would decide to "turn loose." He had a unique laugh, a kind of "he he he he heh," and he was always fooling around with you.

I had seen him castrate pigs on numerous occasions with his pocketknife, which he kept honed as sharp as any razor. Although done when the pigs were small feeder pigs, it took two people to hold the hog. He would make a long slice in the sack just barely deep enough to cut the skin, and the teste and attached tube would drop, and then he simply cut the tube, releasing the teste into his hand. Then the cut would have pine tar applied to each side and be pinched back together. This formed a stitch-free bond that would serve to hold the wound together as well as keep out dirt and ward off infection. It was also just pliant enough to allow the wound to drain and not become infected. He was ahead of his time. I think only in the last few years have doctors started using glue to bind human cuts without using stitches. The pigs, which would let out a sharp squeal when the long incision was made each time, simply "shook it off" and after the deed was finished, off they went back about their business. Pigs are some tough hombres.

He usually just dropped the teste, or "mountain oyster" as he called it, into his pocket. He never charged anyone for the service, just took the mountain oysters as payment. The community was really lucky to have someone like him around. Later Aunt Juanita would wash them, remove the outer skin and tube, split the aforementioned "oyster" in half, batter it in flour, and fry it in a cast-iron pan. No one in the family other than him ate them. (There

137

was one occasion when two people tried them, not knowing what they were, and wanted to throw up when they found out, but I won't mention that here!) I always wondered exactly how he came to "develop his taste for them," yet I never truly wanted to know. Brains and mountain oysters were two foods I did not have a palate for.

Bulls were even more fascinating. You could not hold a bull without risk of injury and Uncle Page had a unique method of castrating them. The bull would be put into a stall where it had limited movement. Uncle Page would quietly get behind it, reach up, and "tickle" the sack by rubbing it with his finger. Almost magically the teste would "drop" into the sack, hanging there like a big rock in a leather sling. With his knife he would make the long incision and again it would drop, and he would cut the tube, pine tar the wound, and repeat. I have seen bulls do nothing more than swish their tails during the whole thing. The secret, he said, was a sharp knife.

His favorite thing was to catch me on the porch facing him in the chair and start a conversation — "What you doing in school, boy?" — and as I would get ready to answer, Uncle Bo would grab my arms from behind and Uncle Page would take out his pocketknife and say, "Time to git 'em." And somehow, even though I knew he was kidding, I always wondered if this would be the time that he *wasn't* kidding. After all everything else lost theirs; I wasn't ever entirely sure I wasn't going to lose mine.

He was fun to be around. He looked and acted the most like Grandaddy, the biggest difference being Grandaddy always wore bib overalls and Uncle Page always wore dark green or dark gray matching work pants and shirt. He chewed tobacco just like Grandaddy. Apple was the brand name both bought if they had money; if not, they simply made twists that looked like a curled pigtail, bit off chunks, and chewed them. Each had a big ceramic spittoon at home that they could accurately hit from a distance if need be.

Uncle Page and Aunt Rachel both shared one common characteristic: if you asked them a question, you would get the answer that was on their mind; they did not sugarcoat anything to anyone. Many times at Hines Store, I would hear Uncle Page tell someone something as bluntly as it could be put and no more, and I

138

would stand and wait for what I was sure was gonna be a mess. But it never happened.

Although after I left home at seventeen, I would see him from time to time over the years, the meetings were seldom and brief. My last real memory was in a tobacco field on a hot muggy day in early September. He, Uncle Bo, and I were pulling tobacco, at his house. I had just been elevated from "unloading the slide" to puller the year before. For lunch Aunt Juanita had fixed the usual tomatoes, corn, snap beans, homemade biscuits, fried middlin', mashed potatoes, and she had cooked a coon. Page and Aunt Juanita, but mostly Uncle Page, probably ate more game than anyone else in the family and she was a master at cooking game.

I felt an unusual kinship with Uncle Page because we both liked raccoon. I don't know the spices it was cooked in, but it was soaked in salt water and vinegar, which would be changed out several times over a period of about twenty-four hours, and then parboiled until fall-off-the-bone tender. Load it up with vinegar and salt, and it had a pleasant taste, plus it was made even more succulent by everyone at the table who said, "I don't see how you eat that." Page and I would have finished it all off.

We were topping the tobacco — pulling off the last of the leaves from the stalk — which would mean tobacco auctions and better times were not far off. It was late afternoon and we had only about six rows to go. We could have easily finished them off and been done with it, but it seems the three of us had somehow had more than our usual share of fun joking around that day and I was "still intact," if you know what I mean. I guess I was sixteen. Uncle Page said he was going to the store for "drinks."

I was about to say, "Git me a Sun-Drop" when he said, "I'm gonna git me a beer, y'all want one?"

At first I thought I was mistaken about the way he meant "y'all"; surely I wasn't included? I really hated the taste of beer, but this was somehow too much to pass up.

I said, "Sure, I'd like one."

Uncle Bo shot me a look but didn't say anything. Page left, and Uncle Bo and I found a shade tree and sat rolling tobacco wax off our hands and saying nothing. About thirty minutes later Uncle Page came back. I'm sure he must have bought a six-pack but he returned with four cans of cold Schlitz and a Pepsi for Bo.

We sat in the glory of the coming sunset and the beer tasted mighty good for the first time ever. Now I understood; it wasn't the beer, it was the company. That was the story of all the laughter at Claude Daniels, the good times going to Dixie's Bridge. It was the company, and on that day it was good company indeed.

Hunter or Hunted

Rain the night before had turned the path heading to the pond into a thick red goo that would have given the famed La Brea Tar Pits a run for their money. My Converse tennis shoes not only were covered, they had been sucked loose so many times, my socks were covered as were my overalls and ankles. Fog had yet to burn off and even though I knew I was on the path; the landscape was eerie. It was early spring, so the bream were bedding. I had an old king mackerel can with the jagged-edge top still sticking up and I would constantly stop and push the escaping "red wiggler" fishing worms back into the dark soil at the bottom.

Almost instinctively I started to whistle, "Bobwhite, bobwhite," the call of the male quail. Immediately I got a "bobwhite" reply from just ahead. I was standing near a large pine tree with low-hanging branches, so I put the worm can down along with my cane pole, climbed the tree, and called again.

"Bobwhite, bob, bobwhite."

Again, an immediate answer, and I was getting excited.

Then I saw him out of the corner of my eye: a large cross fox — part red, part gray — was coming my way, slowly, picking up and placing one foot at a time.

Well, I thought, *that was fun, but I think I've had enough fun. If I whistle "bobwhite" again he will see me and leave.* So I did. But what I got was a "bobwhite" reply and it was behind me! The bird had somehow gone around and behind me while I was looking at the fox. The fox was directly under the tree and smelling the worm can, its ears nervously twitching one at a time, and looking, right, then left, then over its shoulder. All I could think was, *Don't look up.* I couldn't remember if foxes could climb trees!!!

The quail went "bobwhite" and the fox was gone, almost like a mirage. Was he ever there? My heart was pounding. I could hear my every breath. I waited an eternity and on shaky legs climbed down, got the cane pole and worms, and headed to the pond. Still foggy, and now cloudy, it was almost as dark as dusk again.

I don't know if I heard the twig snap first or saw him first, but there he was behind me, the cross fox. I stopped and he stopped, I moved, and he moved. There were no large trees left. I was alone and in the cutover. No need to holler, no one would hear me.

Then it hit me: I would holler at him. Why had I not thought of that? I dropped the worms and pole, raised my arms, and let go with a scream that would wake the dead. Wake the dead maybe, but the fox did not move.

I left the pole and worms, breaking out in a dead run. My left leg slammed into a cut-off branch sticking about twelve inches out from a stump in the cutover. I looked down. There was a hole the size of a dime and a good half-inch deep, and I was bleeding. And then I knew: Of course! He was rabid ... he had to be rabid ... why else would he follow me?

But then I heard it. "Bobwhite," ahead and to my left. When I looked back, the fox was gone. It was the bird; he was still after the bird.

I went back for the worms and the pole, and I went home.

They probably weren't biting anyway.

The Rabbit Box

It was bordering on a whiteout. The snow was blowing sideways, and it was hard to tell the difference between sky and ground. The one-room log cabin had just been finished that year, and dried mud freshly chinked the small gaps between the logs. It was there I was headed with a full load of fur draped over my shoulder. Two coyote, four beaver, a marten, three mink, and a muskrat. All were freshly skinned and fleshed, the best day's catch from the line of leghold traps I was running along the ledge above the river.

But then, like all boyhood dreams, something interrupts them. This time it was the smell of coffee gurgling in the percolator.

I had spent the night at Grandma's house. We had a collection of old, rusted leghold traps from some ancestor who actually had used them, and I remember Grandaddy telling stories of coons that chewed their legs off rather than be trapped.

My Uncle Bo had helped me build a rabbit box, a simple rectangular box with a slotted opening at the front for a door that would rise and fall. That was attached by a nail in its center to some tobacco twine and then to a long thin stick. In the center of the box was a drilled hole into which a "trigger," just a stick with a notch carved in the center, was hooked. From another small nail the trigger was attached to the other end of the same thin stick. Just in front of the drilled hole was another hole into which a peg had been inserted. The long thin stick was placed on top of this peg with the door up, and the notched stick barely holding it, balanced there. The animal, usually a rabbit, would enter the box with the door up, enticed by food, touch the trigger, the door would fall and voilà … rabbit!

Although I was anxious to go check the rabbit box, I was also still groggy, and it was cold. The wood heater would always burn out at night and waking up in an uninsulated wood frame house with floorboards just inches above the dirt was never exciting.

I made my way to the kitchen, where Grandma was standing

in a faded print dress she had made herself, tending the woodstove. We said "good morning" and she reminded me to "Wash up before you eat and put on some clean clothes, before you get on that school bus."

It was pleasantly warm, and the smell of freshly perked coffee and fried middlin' meat was working its charm. I was hungry! I sat down; poured a cup of coffee, with two spoonful's of sugar; and grabbed a thick, fluffy homemade biscuit and slathered it with butter off a home-churned patty Grandma had made just days earlier. Freshly canned pear preserves were ladled on with a big wooden spoon that I had actually carved for her myself from one of the "outsides" of wood down at the barn. Two pieces of middlin' meat cracked in half and added to the center, and the first one was ready to go, anyway. I usually ate until I was told "that's enough for now."

I had set the rabbit box for weeks, down by the barn, at the branch, up by the spring, always in or near thick brambles or honeysuckle, and always … nothing. Uncle Bo had said the human scent had to wear off, and in a streak of brilliance the day before when I had set the box I had rubbed it inside and out with apple peel before placing the peel at the backside.

I guess Daddy was headed for the outhouse; somehow, we crossed paths and he decided to follow me down to the barn. It was cold. I was born blessed with a set of big "Reese ears," as we laughingly called them, and they felt about ready to fall off. My breath would fog so far, I actually tried to see how much distance I could get! As we turned the corner of the mule shed, I could see the door to the box was down!

I felt a rush of excitement like I had never experienced; I was a real fur trapper! We stood the box up on end, with the door facing us and slowly lifted it because we didn't know what was inside. Sure enough it was a rabbit! But … now what?

It was then that I learned the term "rabbit punch" was a real one. Daddy explained, you grab the rabbit by its hind legs, pull it from the box, let it dangle upside down, and then "rap" it as hard as you can just at the back of the head near the neck. That will kill it.

"You show me this time," I said.

"NO, you caught it, you kill it," he said. He started back

toward the house.

I looked at the back of the trap and two big brown eyes, barely blinking looked back at me, helplessly. I reached in, grabbed the back legs, and pulled it out. It made no effort to bite me or hurt me in any way. I made a fist, held it slightly away from me … and … set it on the ground and smacked it on the hind leg. Like a bullet it headed back to the brambles.

God, how I hated eyes. If animals had no eyes, they would be much easier to kill. I think that's why rifles were invented, if you really want to know. So we wouldn't have to see the eyes.

I told Daddy it "jerked out of my hand and got away." I knew that the lie didn't hold, but I also knew that deep down he hadn't wanted to kill it either, and that was somehow a good feeling, even better than the excitement of the catch.

I caught many more rabbits, a raccoon, and a big box turtle, and they all met the same fate. All went free.

But at night, I could still run the traplines. I cured and ate my own jerky, lived off the land, fished, sold fur, and fought Indians and bears. At night. That's where the real magic lay.

BB Gun

As I aligned the sights on the rusted tin can, brightly outlined by the heavy frost of a cold, late January morning, I imagined a fat bobwhite on the receiving end of the cold, blue steel barrel. I had in my hands a brand-new Daisy Pump Action BB Gun. It was my reward for working in tobacco that year. Certainly not the .22-caliber rifle that I had wanted, but a far cry from the old Red Ryder lever action that had seen so many owners over the years. I breathed in, and as I exhaled, I shot the rifle on "empty lungs" as I had been taught, gently squeezing the trigger like "clicking a ballpoint pen." A sharp, metallic "pthwaat" was followed by a light mist of oil pushed by the BB from the freshly lubricated barrel. I walked to my target. Sure enough, dead center of the rusted can was a perfect circular hole on one side and a jagged *V* of metal sticking out on the other.

Man, does this thing have the power, I thought.

I took a stick and retrieved the BB from the dirt pushed up behind the can. BBs were five cents for a bag of 100 at Badeye's and I retrieved every one I could find.

I had gotten up at dawn. It was a school day, but I couldn't sleep and this gave me a little time to unwind before Bus 3 came to force me into the portion of a day that I had come to despise: school. Sharing a biscuit left over from supper, I had bribed Old Bob, Uncle Bo's bird dog, into following me on my journey. Tom, the mule, had come out of his shed and was standing in the rising sun, the steam misting off his neck and back as its warmth relieved him of the night's chill.

Suddenly aware that my teeth were chattering, I looked down in disbelief at my shoes and school pants, wet up to the ankle and a mass of beggar lice and cockle burrs. *No wonder Old Bob didn't want to make the trip; he's no fool*, I thought. I knew I would go to school that way as well; I wasn't about to let Grandma catch me like this. I laughed to myself about having to pick off the "weed seed."

As I rounded the corner of the oldest barn, an ash-gray log

barn chinked with fresh mud every year, a blood-curdling wail that could only come from the souls of the dead pierced the still morning air. It was a screech owl that roosted in the barn most nights. I could see his ghostly eyes and long tufted feathers that looked for all the world like ears, and he was flying right at me, or so it seemed. The big red oak behind the barn had branches that extended toward the front and he had to fly down first before he could fly up and out. Regardless, he had me spooked; hearing a screech owl meant only one of two things: bad news or a death in the family, and I was shaken clean down to the gut. My arms trembled, heart pounded, and I gasped for quick short breaths of air. Somehow, I had ran about twenty yards and as my vision returned to normal, I saw Old Bob who seemed unfazed as he patiently sat and waited for me to "get it together."

We ambled slowly down the red clay path toward the branch. Ice tentacles stuck upward from the clay path and I had to walk the wood's edge to keep from making a crunching noise with every step, even though that was one of my favorite things to do.

Suddenly, seemingly without reason, Old Bob stopped stone cold, his tail was straight out and his right foot slightly raised. But it wasn't without reason; he had located bobwhite. Out of the corner of my eye I saw three quail run … stop … run … stop as they nervously looked around. I slowly raised the rifle, sighted on a big ol' bobwhite and just as I was about to squeeze the trigger I remembered: Damn, I can't shoot quail on the ground. Uncle Bo had told me that time and time again. No one will know I told myself, there's no way they could know. My finger tightened.

No one but you, I thought. *Dammit*. I lowered the rifle.

"Hunt," I told Old Bob, and he jumped in and flushed the quail. So many took flight it was impossible to pick a target, but I blindly shot toward them anyway, in the hope of a miracle … but none was to come. Dejectedly, I started back for the house. Somehow I felt proud just for our finding the birds. And I had done the right thing, even though it would have been a good feeling cradling two bobwhite feet between my thumb and forefinger as I toted the prize back home.

I put the BB gun in the rafters of the chicken house, my "hiding place." A few minutes later Bus 3 was backing into my driveway. As I climbed the steps, wet to the knees still, my eyes gazed at a full bus, not a seat to be seen anywhere. Uncle Clyde had run the route backwards as he sometimes did to break the monotony. The end result of this was my worst nightmare, a full bus; nowhere was there an empty spot to sit. Shuddering, I remembered the screech owl: bad news or a death in the family. There were only two things that could happen.

Momma

This is the story I never wanted to tell, the one that probably drove me to alcohol more than anything else I had experienced. The one that I cry about the most as I write. The one that keeps me up at night sometimes still.

No one lived a sadder life than my Momma, did. I don't know all the details, just bits and pieces. Her father, Henry Gholson, moved a lot, running small rural stores he rented, and cured tobacco in Canada every year. Her momma, whose name I think was Louiza Bolin, was a full-blooded Cherokee Indian. The story, as I was told, was that while at a store in Barnes Junction that he was renting, a man came in to rob the store and killed her mother during the holdup. She witnessed that as a young child. A few years later one of her sisters was shot and killed at a dance in the area. About five years ago, I found their graves in a small, unmarked cemetery off Gholson Road near that store, but before I could investigate much, the land was repurchased and the new owners will not let anyone on it.

Her mental state was never diagnosed or treated way back then. She and Daddy dated, were married, and moved into the house with Granddaddy and Grandma. Uncle Page and Aunt Juanita had married earlier and lived with Grandma and Granddaddy for a while. Uncle Page had then built the small frame two-room house that would later become ours, so he and Aunt Juanita could have some privacy.

Aunt Sis said Momma never seemed comfortable when they stayed with Grandma and Granddaddy, would voice concerns that her "things were being stolen," and seemed to miss home. Granddaddy had punished Aunt Sis once because my Momma said Aunt Sis had stolen Momma's ink pen. Aunt Sis hadn't done it, and denied it, but was punished anyway. The pen was later found.

Uncle Page and Aunt Juanita moved down to Frank Rogers's two-story frame house and started sharecropping. The small two-room house became Momma's and Daddy's.

She became pregnant with me. It may have been postpartum depression, coupled with her mental state at the time, but she could not handle having a child, and my Granddaddy said he would raise me. That is what began the day at Grandma's, night at Daddy's routine that I would live.

There was never food at our house. Ever. The cabinets and refrigerator were always bare of anything but water. Anything we ate, and it was usually just bologna or maybe eggs, my Daddy brought home each night. Usually they ate bologna sandwiches on plain white bread. No vegetables ever. No milk. He would share a beer or two with Momma and that was it. On Saturday he would sometimes buy a deviled crab, or pint of oysters and make oyster stew.

She spent days in that house, months, and years, with nothing to do. No radio, no TV, no company ... nothing. She had only a couple of dresses, was rail thin, and had lost all her teeth, as did my Daddy.

To make things worse she would have times when she didn't want to go to bed or didn't want to go for a ride. And Daddy would tell me, "Go make your Momma come on out." I would ask, beg, plead, but she would not go. But if I yelled, screamed, she would come. I hated doing that; it ate away at me, and yet the more things went downhill, the more I was asked to do it.

I can't describe what it feels like to go through the lunch line at school, even though I worked in the cafeteria every day, in order to even be able to eat lunch, knowing your Momma was at home with nothing coming until supper time. It was an indescribable hurt.

When I was eleven she became pregnant with my brother, Billy. Granddaddy told Daddy he was not going to raise another child. On the night Billy was born she refused to go to the hospital even after her water broke. I was there when that happened and scared to death by it. I was again asked to "make your Momma go to the hospital" and again the screams worked. Once there she said she "would not have the baby." I think she had to be restrained in labor. Dr. Saunders told Daddy he would recommend the baby be taken for adoption if things did not improve.

My Aunt Juanita gave the baby its first bath. My Aunt Sis came over and showed Momma how to boil baby bottles and change diapers and umbilical cord dressings, but she really was just not able to. I remember at eleven years old making sure diapers were changed, making sure he was breathing and on his back.

I couldn't have friends over, couldn't have my parents at any school functions. With Granddaddy gone it seemed we were poorer than ever. I became withdrawn.

This is a story that cannot have a timeline that follows the rest of the chronology; it must end in this one writing. Daddy would eventually move from the small two-room house into the big two-story house Uncle Page lived in. I think Frank Rogers rented it to him for forty dollars a month.

Eventually Momma was taken by the state and placed in what was called the African American Rest Home, or something close to that name, in Richmond.

She took money she saved and bought Daddy a big wide wedding band. It must have cost her a lot because it was real gold. He cherished it and I made sure he was buried with it.

I saw her only twice in all the years she was there. I just couldn't bring myself to go. On one trip I brought her home for a few days' visit and she stayed at Grandma's. She looked better, had gained some weight but she was ready to go back to the home almost as soon as she got there.

My only other visit to see her was the last one. I got a call in 2002 that my Momma had ovarian cancer. I struggled with the visit, but I went. She recognized me and simply said, "Sugar, I hate for you to see me like this." We exchanged small talk for maybe half an hour. ... We were mother and son, and yet were night and day. We did not know each other, on any level. As I was planning a second visit only a week or so later, I got the call that she had passed.

She had no insurance. I was making jewelry at home, the economy was down, and Mary Ann and I were on the verge of losing everything we owned. I could not afford to bury her in a vault, just a water-tight coffin, and still it was $7,000. I felt that even in death somehow life had cheated her. Crowder-Hite-Crews Funeral Home let me make payments until I settled the debt.

I owe my mother for my very life, and yet I never knew her, but God I know how much she suffered. If I could give her my remaining years I would do it. If I could go back in time and change one thing about my life, it would be to give her life; I would make sure she had one. She never did.

WHAT DID IT MEAN?

Where did it go, what did it mean?
All I have spoken, all I have seen,
Memories I shared, with those I loved so,
Like rain they have vanished, where did it go?

Others before me, and others to come
Live life in wonder, love daughter and son,
Their future uncertain, not wanting to know.
What did it mean, where did it go?

What did I miss, what did I lose
Because of decisions, I did not chose?
What love was left waiting, never to know,
No way to blossom, no way to grow?

Paths never taken, hearts never seen
Left now to wonder, what might have been.
Age may give wisdom, but wisdom denies
Feelings that linger, deep there inside.

Life is a mystery, most lies unseen,
Unfolding in rhythm, just like a dream.
Like lightning it passes, in front of our eyes
Then as we grasp it, somehow it dies.

Where did it go, what did it mean?
Why as it passes, do we try to cling?

Our hearts know the answers, but they will not share
All that was possible, all that was there.
Best not to know is what we are told.
As long as there's breath, it still can unfold,
Emotions run deep, they feed on the soul.

Paths never taken, hearts never seen
Left now to wonder, what might have been.

Jimmy Reese

To my readers. . .

I would like to thank all of my readers who have made this memoir possible. The accounts represented here are my memories of true events, as I remember them.

Volume #2 is on the way and will be published soon and will pick up where Streak of Lean left off.

I truly hope you have enjoyed reading these stories.

Made in the USA
Columbia, SC
05 December 2020